Beo   .. and the North before the Vikings

PAST IMPERFECT

See further
www.arc-humanities.org/our-series/pi

Beowulf and the North before the Vikings

Tom Shippey

British Library Cataloguing in Publication Data
A catalogue record for this book is available from the British Library

ISBN (print) 9781802700138
e-ISBN (PDF) 9781802700541
e-ISBN (EPUB) 9781802700558

www.arc-humanities.org
Printed and bound in the UK (by CPI Group [UK] Ltd), USA (by Bookmasters), and elsewhere using print-on-demand technology.

Contents

To Catherine
For unfailing help and support

Preface and Acknowledgements

What follows is a challenge to a well-established consensus, which as I argue below was created in large part by Professor Tolkien. It is also in some respects a dialogue with Tolkien, and moreover points to a kind of dialogue between Tolkien young and Tolkien old—a dialogue which has hardly been noticed within the scholarly world. I am happy to have been able to draw attention to some of Tolkien's later views, and I think he too would have been pleased to have this happen.

I am deeply grateful to many scholars for their help and advice, including John Hines, Leonard Neidorf, Rafael Pascual, and Rolf Bremmer, and particularly so to those who advised me in an area where I am at a considerable disadvantage, namely the archaeology of post-Roman Scandinavia. Frands Herschend, Ole Kastholm, John Ljungkvist, and Martin Rundkvist have all been most generous both in answering my questions, which has given me great encouragement, and in sending me materials which I would otherwise never have seen. Translations are my own, unless otherwise stated, but Stefan Ekman and Rory McTurk helped me out with Swedish. Michael Drout, Nelson Goering, and Sam Newton have read drafts, made comments, and saved me from errors.

Such errors as survive are my own responsibility, and I am also aware that the help I have been given does not imply agreement with my conclusions or suggestions, which I know is sometimes not the case. I hope, nevertheless, that what I have written will encourage others to investigate further what is a notably dark area in both literature and history: though one which has been much and recently illuminated by archaeology.

Introduction

Fantasy or History?

Beowulf is the most enigmatic work in English literature. After more than two hundred years of dedicated study by whole libraries of scholars, we still don't know when or where it was written, who wrote it, what kind of person wrote it, what kind of person it was written for (monks? warriors? kings?), and least of all, what was the point of writing it in the first place.

In fact, it is probably the case that there is *nothing at all* you can say about *Beowulf* that has not been challenged or denied. If you say, "*Beowulf* is a poem," there are immediately voices crying, "No, it is two poems"—or more, the highest bid so far being eleven[1]—"so ineptly joined together that you can still see the stitch-marks!" If you say "*Beowulf* is in Old English," the fact is undeniable, but there are immediately voices raised to say, "It is *now*, but it has to be a translation from some other language"—Old Danish, Old Norse, Old Frisian, the latest contender being Old Gutnish, the language of the Swedish island of Gotland.[2] As for the sentence which

---

1 See T. A. Shippey and Andreas Haarder, eds. and trans., *Beowulf: The Critical Heritage* (London: Routledge, 1998), 67 for the eleven-poems view; and 49 ff. for dissectionism more generally.

2 As proposed by Bo Gräslund, *Beowulfkvädet: Den nordiska bakgrunden* [The Poem Beowulf: The Nordic Background], (Uppsala: Akademien för svensk folkkultur, 2018). An English translation exists as *The Nordic Beowulf*, trans. Martin Naylor (Leeds: Arc Humanities Press, 2022). For other claims about the poem's

begins this Introduction, there has never been any shortage of people who are quite sure they understand the poem perfectly. Only they never agree with each other.

In this cloud of doubt and disagreement, there is nevertheless one opinion held so strongly that it has become an academic article of faith. This is, that *Beowulf*—to quote the Swedish historian Lars Gahrn—is "completely useless for the student of history." *Beowulf* offers a detailed account of early Swedish history, which is consistent with a good deal of early Swedish and Danish legend, but Dr. Gahrn doesn't believe any of it.

He is seconded by Tom Christensen, a Danish archaeologist, who declares that "When historians reject the Lejre legends [of which *Beowulf* is a part], their judgment must be accepted." The view becomes authoritative in the fourth revised edition of Friedrich Klaeber's *Beowulf*, in effect the poem's Authorized Version, where the three modern re-editors state flatly and collectively that "the poem does not offer reliable historical fact." One of them, writing solo, goes on to insist that "The search for genuine history in the Danish episodes of *Beowulf* is the search for a chimera."[3]

That would appear to be that. The strange thing is that these strong and insistent statements are often accompanied by tiny murmurs of doubt. In his very distinguished PhD thesis from Cambridge, Carl Edlund Anderson makes the obligatory profession of faith—doctoral theses are not a good

---

original provenance / language, see again Shippey and Haarder, *Beowulf: The Critical Heritage*, 61, 131, 376.

3 See respectively Lars Gahrn, *Sveariket i källor och historieskrivning* [Sweden in the Sources and the Writing of History] (Göteborg: Historiska institutionen, 1988), 281; Tom Christensen, "Lejre: Fact and Fable," in *Beowulf and Lejre*, ed. Niles and Osborn, 13–101 at 82 (full citation to this collection in Further Reading); *Beowulf*, ed. F. Klaeber, revised as *Klaeber's Beowulf, 4th Edition*, ed. R. D. Fulk, Robert E. Bjork and John D. Niles (Toronto: Toronto University Press, 2008), li; Niles, "Beowulf and Lejre," in *Beowulf and Lejre*, ed. Niles and Osborn, 169–233 at 225.

place to go challenging established opinion—by saying, "it can hardly be stressed enough that doubt surrounding the origins of Beowulf's narrative argues strongly against the use of it...as a historical source." He also notes, however, on the same page but one feels in a rather quieter voice, how well the poem appears to fit "the pattern of Scandinavian history." Similarly, the Klaeber editors, having laid down the law, concede disapprovingly that "the poem does present an air of reality and truth,"[4] though they don't say how this comes about. Although Professor Christensen is prepared to "reject the Lejre legends," if told to do so by historians, his own excavations have very strongly confirmed those legends in one point which was regarded not long ago as total fantasy, see further pp. 34–36 below.

The poem, in short, is generally agreed to be completely unreliable historically, but at the same time insidiously, even dangerously, convincing. To borrow a sentence from Professor Tolkien, "There is something irritatingly odd about all this."[5] Even odder is the fact that this is largely Tolkien's fault.

All Tolkien's Fault?

On November 25, 1936 Tolkien read a lecture to the British Academy in London, with the title, "*Beowulf*: the Monsters and the Critics." Once published, it changed the whole course of *Beowulf*-criticism: it is said to be the most-quoted and most-cited academic article ever written in the field of English literature. Its intention was and is perfectly clear. Tolkien insisted that the poem must be taken on its own merits; that fantasy

---

4 Carl Edlund Anderson, "Formation and Resolution of Ideological Contrast in the Early History of Scandinavia" (PhD diss., University of Cambridge, 1999), 56; *Klaeber's Beowulf, 4th Edition*, ed. Fulk et al., li.

5 J. R. R. Tolkien, "*Beowulf*: The Monsters and the Critics," *Proceedings of the British Academy* 32 (1936): 245–95 at 254. (What Tolkien thought was so odd was the critical belief that the poet had focused on *the wrong things*, i.e., the monsters.)

was an entirely legitimate literary genre; and that he much preferred "the monsters" to "the critics."

In doing so, he was not only starting a new tradition in *Beowulf*-studies, he was also rejecting an old one. *Beowulf* became known to the modern world in 1815, when the first edition of it was published in Copenhagen. It immediately became of great interest to scholars, especially German scholars, working in the century during which Germany became a unified nation. In some ways it was just what they wanted: a very early epic, which if not German was at least in a Germanic language, and imbued with heroic spirit.

In other ways, however, it was very disappointing. It was at bottom a fairy-tale, about a hero, a troll, a water-hag, and a dragon, and even the hero looked like the hero of a fairy-tale, specifically the tale of "The Bear's Son"—Beowulf is terribly strong, not much use with swords, and opts to fight (no pun intended) bare-handed. German scholars wanted something more human-oriented, more traditionally heroic, more like *The Iliad* or (even better) *The Nibelungenlied*. Since *Beowulf* was all they had, however, they set about rewriting it, cutting out bits they didn't like, and treating the poem as the ruin of a much better poem behind it which unfortunately hadn't survived.

Tolkien, quite correctly, thought this was ridiculous. When in 1936 he wrote, sarcastically, that "It would really have been preposterous" if the poet had "told of [Beowulf's] cleansing of Heorot, and then brought him to defeat in a... Swedish invasion,"[6] he was probably thinking of a scholar who had just argued for pretty much that, the dogged but unfortunate Walter Berendsohn, who brought out his book on "the prehistory of *Beowulf*" earlier that same year.[7] Tolkien was right: this was a scholarly tradition that deserved to die. Tolkien was also quite right to say that the poem deserved to be

6 Tolkien, "*Beowulf*: The Monsters and the Critics," 276.

7 For Berendsohn's near-tragic career, see again Shippey and Haarder, *Beowulf: The Critical Heritage*, 69–71. Berendsohn could stand as an exemplar of the nationalist tradition against which Tolkien was reacting, so extreme as to be almost allegorical.

taken on its own merits, not compared with something more desirable that didn't exist, and his lead has been followed ever since.

One might, however, sound two notes of caution. The first is obvious. If there was one person in the world with a personal motive for defending the legitimacy of fantasy, who was it but Tolkien? He had been writing fantasy about goblins and elves and dragons (in secret) for twenty years, and had in fact, as he read his ground-breaking lecture on November 25, 1936, just started the process of going public by sending his typescript of *The Hobbit* to a publisher not quite two months earlier.

The other note of caution is that Tolkien was perfectly capable of an element of guile (especially if he thought it was funny, and note the comic element of his lecture-title). In that lecture, at one point—arguing that dragons were just as good a subject for literature as heroes—he told his learned audience that "More than one poem in recent years...has been inspired by the dragon of *Beowulf*."[8] This was literally true. There *had* been more than one poem. There had been two. One was written by Tolkien himself, the other by C. S. Lewis, and we know this because in his early drafts of the lecture—now edited by Michael Drout—he wrote both poems out in full.[9] So what Tolkien was really saying was, "Well, anyway, *I like dragons*...and what's more, *so does my best friend!*" But his learned audience might not have found this totally convincing as evidence of a collective taste.

All this must cast some doubt on Tolkien's rejection of the-poem-as-history. Right at the start of his lecture Tolkien declared that "The illusion of historical truth and perspective...is largely a product of art," going on to warn that "the seekers after history must beware lest the glamour of Poesis

---

8 Tolkien, "*Beowulf*: The Monsters and the Critics," 258.

9 Michael Drout, *Beowulf and the Critics, by J. R. R. Tolkien* (Tempe: Arizona Center for Medieval and Renaissance Studies, 2002), 56–58 and 110–14.

overcome them."[10] His statement and his warning have ever since been swallowed whole. But it is a pity that Tolkien (and his followers) have never bothered to explain exactly how this "literary art" and "glamour of Poesis" actually work to create conviction, though even the Klaeber editors admit that the "air of reality and truth" is there.

In any case, we now know, from his posthumous publications, that Tolkien was kidding—and not just about dragons. In reality, when he wasn't, for his own reasons, making the case for fantasy, he took *Beowulf*-as-history very seriously indeed. After eighty-five years, it's time his 1936 opinion was challenged.

Two Solid Facts (At Last): I, A Young Man and an Old One

Beowulf's anti-historical critics do of course have a point. If you believe that history cannot be written without dates and documents, then *Beowulf* offers neither. On the other hand, students of prehistory are accustomed to making what they can of other kinds of evidence, like legends and late traditions. And there is in addition the solid and ever-increasing evidence of archaeology, the "open frontier" of *Beowulf*-studies and of early history. As Ulf Näsman, Professor of Archaeology at Linnaeus University in Sweden, puts it: "archaeologists can write history."[11] Moreover, and as it happens, even for *Beowulf* we do have some surprising documentary evidence, which also gives us a date.

There are accordingly two things of which we can be sure (as sure as anything can be in this area).

---

10 Tolkien, "*Beowulf*: The Monsters and the Critics," 247, 248.

11 Ulf Näsman, "The Ethnogenesis of the Danes and the Making of a Danish Kingdom," in *Anglo-Saxon Studies in Archaeology and History 10, Papers from the 47th Sachsensymposium (York 1996)*, ed. Tania Dickinson and David Griffiths (Oxford: Oxford University Committee for Archaeology, 1999), 1–10 at 1.

One is that the single copy of the poem, on which all later editions, translations, and commentary depend, was written down close to the year 1000. We can be sure it was a copy, even a copy of a copy, and not the author's own original text, because it makes so many mistakes, some natural, some careless. As for the date, this is fixed by the fact that the copy was written out by two different scribes, who used different handwriting styles. Many Anglo-Saxon manuscripts, such as charters, are legal documents which can be dated, so the handwriting styles can be dated as well. The first scribe of *Beowulf*, scribe A, wrote in a style called English Vernacular Minuscule: this only began to be used after the year 1001, so our copy must be later than that. The second scribe, scribe B, who took over in the middle of a sentence in line 1939, wrote a version of English Square Minuscule, which is not found after 1010, so our copy must be earlier than that.[12]

It's somehow typical of *Beowulf* that while one might expect an older man to die or become disabled and hand over to a younger one, in fact, with *Beowulf*, it's the other way round: perhaps the younger man, scribe A, got promoted from the copying job, and scribe B was called out of retirement to take over. Nevertheless, the poem must have been copied out, surely in a monastic scriptorium (what interest did it have for monks?), in or very close to the decade 1000–1010.

The Other Solid Fact: 2, A King, and a Date

The second and vital fact for this book's argument is that the poem is set in Scandinavia during the sixth century. We know this because of one character only, a man called (in the poem as we have it) Hygelac. He turns out to be Beowulf's uncle, though this only emerges, and then only incidentally, at line 1923, by which time he has been mentioned many times: the poet seems to have thought he didn't need to introduce this character, as everyone in his original audience would know who he was. Also mentioned repeatedly, and with increasing

---

12 See *Klaeber's Beowulf, 4th Edition*, ed. Fulk et al., xxvii.

amounts of detail, is how Hygelac died. He mounted a pirat-
ical raid from what is now south Sweden to what is now the
Netherlands, but was met by a Frankish army, defeated, and
killed with most or all of his men. (The poem says that Beowulf
got away by swimming home, carrying thirty suits of armour
so they would not be looted by the victors: almost no-one has
believed this, though of course someone has tried to explain
it away. One might as well say from the start that everything
to do with the character Beowulf looks like fiction.)

Fortunately for us, however, the Hygelac disaster was
recorded in writing not far from the date of the event by a
Frankish historian, Gregory of Tours.[13] Gregory gives the
name of the raid-leader as "Chlochilaicus," which is not a bad
shot at what Hygelac's name would have been back then,
namely *Hugilaikaz, with the medial -l added through Gregory's familiarity with Frankish names like Chlodomer, Chlo-
dovald. (The asterisk before Hugilaikaz indicates that this
name has been "reconstructed" from what we know about
language-history and language-changes.) Gregory also says
that the raid took place in the reign of King Theuderic, that
is, 511–534. However the Frankish army was led by his son,
Prince Theudebert, who must have been old enough to be
entrusted with the leadership of an army. This argues that
Hygelac was killed rather late in Theuderic's reign, probably
some time after about 525.[14]

Gregory's account, written some time before 594, is confirmed by another Frankish chronicler, the anonymous author
of the *Liber historiae Francorum*. Like Gregory, he wrote in Latin,

---

13 Bk. 3, chap. 3 of Gregory of Tours, *The History of the Franks*,
trans. Lewis Thorpe (Harmondsworth: Penguin, 1974), 163–64.

14 Almost all we know about Theudebert is that he must have
been born before 511, and was first regarded as marriageable
ca. 530, see R. W. Chambers, *Beowulf: An Introduction to the Study
of the Poem with a Discussion of the Stories of Offa and Finn*, 3rd
ed. with a supplement by C. L. Wrenn (Cambridge: Cambridge
University Press, 1959), 381–82, 385–87. 525 is commonly given
as the date of Hygelac's death, but I think ca. 530 is more likely.

and more than a hundred years later (ca. 727), but he adds a few details not found in Gregory, notably the name of the tribe being raided: the *Attoarii*, which corresponds quite well with the tribal name given in *Beowulf*, the *Hetware*. (It should be noted that the Latin alphabet had no letter representing the sound -w, which is why we now write it as a double v, and call the letter "double u." Anglo-Saxon scribes sometimes wrote -uu, but both *Beowulf* scribes sensibly followed normal practice and used the runic letter representing -w from their own native alphabet. The guttural Germanic initial H- also caused Latin scribes confusion: sometimes they dropped it, wrongly, as with the *Attoarii*, sometimes they added it, likewise wrongly, as with the *(H)Eruli*, see p. 23 below.)

Finally, Hygelac was also remembered in England, for he is listed in the English *Liber monstrorum*, or "Book of Monsters," compiled about the same time as the *Liber historiae Francorum*, very likely in Malmesbury.[15] Hygelac is counted as a monster because he was a giant: he was so big, the *Liber* says, that the Franks who killed him kept his skeleton on display on an island in the mouth of the Rhine.[16]

So Hygelac was real, he died ca. 530, he is still alive and well in the first two-thirds of *Beowulf*, but dead long before Beowulf dies fighting the dragon. But the poem was copied ca. 1000. There is then a gap of more than 400 years between the events of the poem and our copy being made, and *Beowulf* was actually written some time in those four long centuries, but we don't know when. (For what it's worth, opinion has recently shifted back to what Tolkien thought: the poem was written ca. 700–725.)[17]

---

15 As argued by M. Lapidge, "*Beowulf*, Aldhelm, the *Liber Monstrorum* and Wessex," *Studi medievali*, ser. 3, 23 (1982): 151–92.

16 All three accounts of the Hygelac raid—Gregory, the *Liber historiae Francorum*, and the *Liber monstrorum*—are given in the original Latin by Chambers, *Beowulf: An Introduction to the Study of the Poem*, 3–4.

17 See *The Dating of Beowulf: A Reassessment*, ed. Leonard Neidorf (Woodbridge: Boydell & Brewer, 2014), *passim*.

A King and a Problem: Who Was He King of?

It is again typical of *Beowulf* that as soon as you get an established fact, you get a problem, or a contradiction, that goes along with it, in this case the question of Hygelac's ethnicity. Beowulf himself belongs to the tribe of the *Geatas*. The second thing we are told about him is that he is *god mid Geatum*, "the good man among the Geats," while the first thing we are told about him is that he is *Higelaces þegn*, "the thane of Hygelac." Just to make sure, the first thing Beowulf actually says himself is that he and his companions are "men of the race of the Geats and the hearth-companions of Hygelac."

Hygelac, then, must have been King of the Geats, a point confirmed in detail later on in the poem. The English *Liber monstrorum* agrees: *Et sunt [monstra] mirae magnitudinis: ut rex Huiglaucus qui imperavit Getis et a Francis occisus erat*, "there are monsters of great size: like king Huiglaucus who ruled the *Getae* and was killed by the Franks." The two Frankish chroniclers, however, disagree. Gregory writes that the attack was made by *Dani cum rege suo nomine Chlochilaico*, "the Danes with their king Chlochilaicus," and the *Liber historiae Francorum* repeats the identification almost word-for-word.

So who was right, the two English writers or the two Frankish ones? The argument in favour of the Franks is that Gregory's account, written before 594 and within living memory of the event, is the earliest report, and it is a good rule to prioritize the earliest evidence. The argument against this is that it is much easier to imagine Geats being mistaken for Danes than the other way round. There is a strong tendency for unfamiliar peoples to be lumped together under the name of the ones who first became familiar. Thus the Romans called all seaborne raiders *Saxones*, and the Celts of Britain followed suit—as they do to this day, the Welsh calling the English *Saeson* and the Scots *Sassenach*. (Harassed provincials were unlikely to hang around questioning whether the thugs who had just landed were indeed Saxons, or Angles, or Jutes, or anyone else: "Saxons" would do for all of them.)

FANTASY OR HISTORY?   11

In just the same way, "Danes" became a catch-all term. The first report of a Viking Age disturbance in England makes the point. The *Anglo-Saxon Chronicle* entry for 789 recording an event at Portland in Dorset, reads:

> three ships of Northmen first came from Hordaland. The king's reeve rode there and wanted to compel them to go to the king's town because he did not know what they were, and they killed him. These were the first ships of the Danish men which sought out the land of the English.[18]

The Chronicler knew quite well that the malefactors were "Northmen," i.e., Norwegians, and even that they came from Horthaland, the area round Bergen, far to the north of even the northern tip of Denmark. Still, as far as he was concerned, all seaborne nuisances were the same: they were all "Danes," and all as bad as each other.

Probably, then, the Frankish chroniclers took the same attitude. The solid and consistent view, in *Beowulf*, that Hygelac ruled the *Geatas*, is much more remarkable, for the fact is that this people was almost completely unknown elsewhere in English records: even the *Liber monstrorum* has borrowed the form *Getis* from *Getae*, a tribe mentioned fairly often in Classical accounts, but hardly if at all connected to historical Scandinavia.

So who were Beowulf's people, the Geats (pronounced "yay-ats")? Scholars were for once fairly agreed on this, at least during the twentieth century. Old English *-ea* corresponds regularly to Old Norse *-au*, as in the words for "red" (OE *read*, ON *rauðr*), the OE plural ending *-as* corresponds even more regularly to ON plural ending *-ar*, the soft OE *G-* again corresponds to the hard ON *G-*, and putting all those together, OE *Geatas* must be the same as ON *Gautar*.

And the *Gautar* remained quite familiar to Scandinavians, as they still are. They are the inhabitants of what are now the two Swedish provinces of Öster- and Väster-götland (in

---

18 *The Anglo-Saxon Chronicle*, trans. Michael Swanton (London: Phoenix, 2000), 54: MS A 787 (for 789).

English, East and West Gothland), which span south-central Sweden from the west coast facing the North Sea to the east coast on the Baltic, the capital of West Gothland being, of course, Götaborg, in English, Gothenburg. So the *Geatas* of *Beowulf* come from Gothland in Sweden, which fits very well with the fact that Beowulf and his companions arrive in Denmark by sea, apparently after no more than a short voyage.

So far so good, but very recently a different view has been put forward, by Bo Gräslund, of Uppsala University: that actually, the *Geatas* came, not from East and West Gothland, on the Swedish mainland, but from the island of Gotland, off the east coast of Sweden.[19] Professor Gräslund thinks that some of the details given about Beowulf's home fit Gotland, for instance the mention of the "sea-wall" near Beowulf's burial-place: there is a prominent sea-wall in Gotland.

Particularly interesting is his explanation of what seems to be an alternative title for the Geats, the *Wederas*: they are called the *Weder-Geats* three times in the poem, and the Danish coastguard assumes that Beowulf and his men will go home *to Wedermearce*, "to Weder-mark." This has generally been taken to mean "weather," so "storm," so perhaps "storm of battle"—"Storm-Geats" would be another self-flattering term like "Spear-Danes." Professor Gräslund, however, argues that *weder* can mean "ram." The Old English word is actually *weðer*, not *weder*, but *ð/d* confusion is common enough; and in modern non-standard English both "wedder" and "wether" continue to be used for a male sheep, usually a castrated male sheep, but still, a ram. And the ram is, and has been since time immemorial, the emblem of the island of Gotland. So maybe the *Weder-Geatas* were actually the Ram-Geats, from Gotland?

The main objection to this theory is not verbal but logistical. In *Beowulf* it is clear that the *Geatas* are one of the major powers of Scandinavia, capable of standing toe-to-toe with the Swedes and (sometimes) defeating them. Gotland has a land area of not quite 1200 square miles, little more than

19 Gräslund, *Beowulfkvädet* / trans. as *The Nordic Beowulf*.

a seventh of the land area of the two Gothland provinces, with a population even more disproportionate. Things were no doubt different 1500 years ago, but the figures still do not seem enough for a major power.

Furthermore in the poem the Geats fight the Swedes *ofer wid wæter*, "across the wide water" (line 2473) and this seems a better description of the great lakes which form the northern border of the modern Gothland provinces than of the channel which divides the island of Gotland from the mainland (and see further p. 57 below). And, of course, one thing that seems fairly sure is that the Geats mounted a major attack on the Frankish kingdom—something much more easily done from Gothenburg than from Gotland: in the Viking Age Gotland was firmly connected not with raiders to the west, but with the river-trade in the east, and down to Byzantium.

One final point is that the Geats, or *Gautar*, or *Götar* in modern Swedish, were at some point assimilated into greater Sweden. But we do not know when the assimilation of *Svenskar* and *Götar* took place. At the end of *Beowulf*, it is looked forward to with foreboding.

The Structure of the Poem

There is a third fact to go along with the date of our copy and the date of Hygelac's fall, but it is one internal to the poem rather than external.

Scholars noticed immediately that the poem is in two parts: at line 2200 the action shifts suddenly fifty years, from Beowulf as a young warrior in Denmark to Beowulf as an old king in Sweden. It is also obvious that the main action of the poem consists of Three Great Fights, two in the first part (Grendel and his mother) and one in the second (the dragon).

Before, after, and in between the Fights, however, we have sections which consist very largely of retrospect, proph- esy, and historical comment. And our third fact is that the poet *allots more space to these than to the pure fantasy of the fights*. Thus:

- in lines 661–836, Beowulf fights Grendel the man-eater in the hall of Heorot (this section is marked in the manuscript as "fitts" XI and XII).

- in lines 1250–1650 (fitts XVIIII–XXIII), Grendel's mother comes to avenge her son (and retrieve his torn-off arm which has been nailed up as a trophy), but is pursued to her underwater lair, and killed with a giant sword.

- in lines 2510–2845 (not marked off in the manuscript) Beowulf advances to fight the dragon, and eventually kills it with the aid of his relative Wiglaf.

The fights then occupy rather less than thirty percent of the poem. Meanwhile:

- in lines 1–660, we are given a genealogy of the Danish kings from Scyld to Hrothgar; told about the hall Heorot; and introduced to Beowulf; while there is a long section in which different accounts are given (one hostile, one defensive) of an earlier exploit by Beowulf.

- lines 837–1249 are pivotal for the poem and change its mood. Beowulf is compared with the great heroes Sigemund and Heremod; rewards are handed out; and a poet sings the story of "the fight at Finnsburg," an earlier triumph for the Danes against the Frisians. The mood of celebration, however, is contradicted by two glimpses of the future. Hrothgar, in the joy of his heart, adopts Beowulf as a son. This does not go down well with his wife, Queen Wealhtheow, who has sons of her own to consider. The question arises of who will succeed King Hrothgar, who is very old. Also, Wealhtheow, apparently anxious to conciliate Beowulf, gives him a large and splendid gold neck-ring. But in a first mention of the Hygelac disaster, we are told that this will be taken from Hygelac's body (Beowulf had passed it on) when Hygelac is killed by the Franks.

- lines 1650 to 2199 continue the mood of foreboding. Hrothgar gives a long speech, the burden of which is, "You never know..." Beowulf and Hrothgar part, each man gving the other a veiled warning, which both ignore. Beowulf reports to Hygelac on return about events at the Danish court, saying that Hrothgar's diplomatic peace-keeping initiative towards his hereditary enemies the Bards won't work.

- at line 2200 the poet then shifts abruptly to Beowulf's old age in Sweden, mentions the Hygelac disaster again, and starts to tell the long story of the Swedish wars, in which the whole royal dynasty of the Geats will be killed, apart from Beowulf, who eventually succeeds to the throne. And then, at line 2211, the dragon comes. As Beowulf advances to meet it, we're told more about the Swedish wars, which have dominated his later life, and Beowulf himself adds more family history, with further details about the Hygelac disaster, reviewing his own warlike career, and we might think, psyching himself up for the dragon. Even during the fight, the action stops for an important historical flashback, lines 2606–30, giving the backstory of the sword Wiglaf draws.

- Finally, with Beowulf and the dragon both dead, in lines 2845 to the end, an unnamed Messenger tells Beowulf's retinue that they have lost their king, reminds them that they have deadly enemies in the Franks and the Swedes, gives a very spirited account of old battles in the Swedish wars, and then says, to put in bluntly, that now they are for the chop. The poet comments, rubbing it in, *he ne leag fela*, "he was not far wrong." Beowulf is lamented, and buried.

Even from this summary one can see, first, that while the three action sequences are upbeat, the passages that frame them are increasingly downbeat. Moreover, just by line-count, the poet seems to have taken more trouble over the historical background (seventy percent plus) than he did over the fantastic foreground (thirty percent minus).

One sign of this is the way he uses names. The three action sequences are as near nameless as one could well imagine. We have Beowulf and Grendel. Grendel's mother's name is not given. The great Danish scholar N. F. S. Grundtvig thought that the adjective *stearcheort* was actually the name of the dragon, and a good name for a dragon it would be, "Stark-heart": but no-one believes him. That apart, we are told the name of Grendel's victim, Hondscio—that is, "Hand-shoe," meaning "glove," a very odd name indeed. Also the name of Grendel's mother's victim Æschere, as well as (for some unknown reason) the name of Æschere's younger brother Yrmenlaf. In the dragon fight Beowulf is rescued by his relative Wiglaf, son of Weohstan, son of Wægmund, also said to be "the kinsman of Ælfhere," while in a strange historical flashback in the very middle of the dragon fight we also hear of the Swedish prince Eanmund. Nine names apart from Beowulf, one weird (Hondscio), one pointless (Yrmenlaf), three seemingly irrelevant (Wiglaf's kinsmen, and these moreover, like Eanmund, in the historical flashback).

The framing sections, however, give us more than sixty names (we aren't always sure what's a name and what isn't). Many of these are as far as we know likewise irrelevant—does it help to know that Heardred was "the kinsman of Hereric"? Maybe it would if we knew who Hereric was. But many are highly significant, even to people with our limited knowledge. As soon as Beowulf tells Hygelac that Hrothgar's daughter Freawaru (never mentioned in any other legend) is betrothed to "the fortunate son of Froda," alarm-bells ring for anyone who knows anything about Germanic legend. The failed revenge of Ingeld son of Froda (Ingeld's name is given just a few lines later) was both famous and much-admired by revenge-fans: Ingeld remained a popular name for real people both in northern England and in Icelandic saga.

The twenty-three names given for members of the royal houses of the Danes, Swedes, and Geats—some known elsewhere like Hygelac and Hrothulf, some completely unrecorded like Freawaru and Hæthcyn—are important as well, even vital. They are also real names, if unfamiliar. The name of Beowulf's father Ecgtheow was never borne, as far as we know, by any other Anglo-Saxon (and we know an awful lot of Anglo-Saxon names), but its exact cognate or parallel turns up in Old Norse, Eggthér: the poet didn't make it up. See the further comment on the name Heorogar, p. 51 below.

Briefly, then, the framing passages of the poem, so often overlooked, are packed with information, and even if we can't understand it, the poet thought that information was important. That is because he was talking about politics.

Chapter 1

Poetry and Archaeology

Smashed Halls and Mead-Benches...

So much should have been evident from the first few lines of the poem. They go, in the manuscript, lines 1–6a, before editors got to work on them:

> Well, we have heard of the power, in far-off days, of the people-kings of the Spear-Danes, how the princes performed glorious deeds. Scyld Scefing often took away the mead-benches (*meodosetla*) from troops of enemies, from many tribes, he struck fear into the warrior (*egsode eorl*).

[Note that Scyld means "shield" and was pronounced more or less like the modern word, while Scefing means either "son of Sheaf," again pronounced more or less like the modern word, or else, "with a sheaf": we don't know which, and neither makes much sense.]

Two things, nevertheless, are obvious right away. First, the poet clearly thinks his original audience (whoever they were) *had* heard of the old Danish kings. We, on the other hand, the modern audience, haven't—unless informed by two hundred years of scholarly researches. There is a big gap between the poet's "we" and our "we."

Second, something has already gone wrong. Everything in those few lines is plural, princes and benches, troops and tribes, up to the last word, *eorl*, which is singular, and a complete anti-climax. Editors almost always do the obvious thing and just make it plural, *eorlas*, "he struck fear into the warriors." It looks as if there was a gap already between the poet and scribe A, making his copy as much as three hundred years later.

In between we have the strange remark about taking away the mead-benches, or mead-settles (a settle is a bench with a back to it). Nothing like this has ever turned up in any other text from the old Germanic north. However, it's not difficult to understand. The place for mead-settles is in a mead-hall, and a mead-hall (also a wine-hall and no doubt a beer-hall for those on the cheaper benches) is the place for convivial drinking and male-bonding.

The bonding moreover is done between the king, or the leader, and his retinue, his strike-force or armed male supporters. As is very clear from *Beowulf* itself, the hall is where these men drink, gossip, hear the news. It is also where visitors are received, announcements are made, rewards are given, prestige recognized and increased. It is the administrative as well as the social centre of the community. To quote Frands Herschend, Professor of Archaeology at Uppsala University, who has researched Scandinavian halls intensively, "one cannot be a leader without a hall."[1]

Leader, note, not necessarily king. The communities served by a hall need not have been big ones. Line 2 of *Beowulf* mentions "people-kings" (*þeodcyninga*), and in Old Norse, at least, a strong distinction is made between "people-kings" (*þjóðkonungar*) and "little-kings" (*smákonungar*). Even little-kings must have had halls, though. Kings and halls go together, even more than halls and leaders.

So what does "taking away the mead-settles" mean? It means that the mead-hall is being taken out of commission, and that in turn means that its owner has been displaced—and that the community he ruled, whatever it was, has lost its independence. The poet is describing, colourfully and economically, a rolling-up process. The people-kings of the Spear-Danes, also known as the Scyldings ("Shieldings" in

I Frands Herschend, "Halle," in *Reallexikon der germanischen Altertumskunde* (Berlin: De Gruyter, 1999), 13:414–25 at 420.

modern English, *Skjöldungar* in Old Norse), are taking over the smaller or weaker groups, the Brondings, Helmings, Wylfings, and telling the former leaders and their retinues, "from now on you will drink *my* mead, in *my* mead-hall, and be loyal to *me*." They were, to put it briefly, re-focusing loyalties by getting formerly separate groups to drink together, and thus creating a new identity—eventually, a national rather than a tribal one.

This need not have been a violent process. Hrothgar's queen is a woman of the Helmings. His door-warden is Wulfgar, "a man of the *Wendle*," known to Romans as the Vandals, and probably coming from Vendil in North Jutland, a long way from Heorot. On the other hand, most of the time it probably *was* violent, which is obviously what the first few lines of the poem are saying. This violent process has left traces archaeologically, in the form of "smashed halls."

According to Professor Herschend again, these are quite common in Scandinavia, mostly in the southern parts: cases have been located at Dejbjerg and Dankirke in Denmark, at Helgo and Eketorp in Sweden, as well as Borg in Lofoten in the far north of Norway.[2] The process may even have been ritualized, as if there was a ceremonial element in the smashing. At Uppåkra 1 in southern Sweden—a site datable to ca. 500—broken weapons suggest that the victors collected and broke the weapons of the losers before depositing them next to the destroyed hall, thus "combin[ing] battlefield and sacrifice as the manifestation of the end of an era." On several sites, what's been found are glass shards and fragments, sometimes—as at the hall in Lofoten—in the post-holes left after the building's supports had been pulled down, then covered with turf from the fallen roof, all of which suggests "a small series of non-accidental steps taken to destroy the hall." There and elsewhere, someone went to the trouble of breaking up glass drinking bowls—would it not have been more normal just to take these expensive items away? But

---

2 Herschend, *The Idea of the Good*. Some twenty halls are listed in Appendix 1, 182–85.

no: "smashing the glasses went hand in hand with pulling down the buildings."[3]

What the archaeological record suggests, in short, is that for once loot was not the purpose of what was done. Instead, Professor Herschend argues, "the struggle for power among the leading families was to a certain degree a matter of fighting each other with the purpose of destroying each other's halls. Smashing rather than plundering was the keynote of this kind of political rather than economic warfare." Putting it another way, power-struggles among the elite were aimed above all "at reducing the number of prominent hall-owners," who were, to their competitors, so many unwanted potential petty kings.[4] So, pull down their mead-halls, break their mead-cups, destroy their independence—and take away their mead-settles.

Going back to *Beowulf*, it would make sense, actually, not just to take the mead-settles away, but to set fire to them, a process which would leave no archaeological traces. But perhaps the Scylding kings needed the benches themselves, because after all their purpose was to expand their power by building up a much bigger retinue? It's striking that the first thing we learn about Hrothgar is that he decided to build a really big mead-hall, "bigger than the children of men had ever heard of" (lines 69–70). Of course he did, by this time he had a really big retinue to house, his own Scyldings and all the other groups as well!

But some will say this is pure coincidence…as is the fact that a mead-hall which fits the bill has been found exactly where legend said it was, by Professor Christensen, as pointed out on p. 3 above (and see further pp. 34–36 below).

---

3 All quotes above are from Herschend, respectively *Early Iron Age*, 375 (Uppåkra); private communication (Lofoten); "Halle," p. 420 (smashing the glass); *Idea of the Good*, 37 (political warfare); *Early Iron Age*, 369 (reducing the number).

4 Respectively, Herschend, *Idea of the Good*, 37, and *Early Iron Age*, 369.

So much, then, for the mead-settles of line 5 and the smashed halls that go with them. But what went wrong with line 6 and the anti-climax of *egsode eorl*?

...and a Misunderstanding

Almost all editors just pluralize *eorl* to *eorlas*. The problem with that is working out why scribe A would mis-copy a word as normal and familiar as *eorlas*, which has been in the language from that day to this—it means "earls," at that time "nobles, warriors, men of the military upper class"?

Perhaps what he saw in front of him, in the text he was slowly copying—and which he had not yet got to grips with, as one can see from other early mistakes—did not read *eorlas* but *eorle*. Scribe A looked at it, thought (more or less) "that's wrong, *eorle* is dative singular of *eorl*, but the verb *egsode* takes the accusative, I'll correct it." (Scribe A, we know, corrected words one at a time. He did not think about the overall sense of a sentence.)

But Anglo-Saxons, unlike us, did not capitalize proper names. So perhaps what the poet originally meant was *Eorle*, a tribal name, the plural form of which ends in -*e*, just like *Dene*, *Engle*, *Seaxe*, *Wendle*: the Danes, Angles, Saxons, Vandals, and many others. That makes sense. The poet meant the people known to the Romans as the *Heruli* (Latin writers, as said above, were never sure about Germanic *H-*, sometimes adding it, sometimes removing it).

The Heruli were, to put it briefly, the barbarians' barbarians. They were famous for their height, for fighting without helmets or armour, and for their kindly habit of killing any of their male relatives who survived to old age, to spare them the terrible shame of dying a natural death. They had *something* to do with the Danes. The Roman historian Jordanes, writing ca. 550, reports that the Danes drove the Heruli from their homes (*Dani...Herulos propriis sedibus expulerunt*); while the Byzantine Procopius, writing at almost exactly the same time, reports further that many who had been operating as raiders / mercenaries in the Classical world re-emigrated to Scandinavia, passed through Danish territory, and were allowed to re-settle, though we don't know where.[5] Even this indicates that the Heruli/*Eorle* were subordinate to the Danes.

If these are the people indicated in line 6, then one has to say that *Beowulf* opens not with a limp descent into bathos but with a strong and proud assertion. As Gwyn Jones puts it in his *History of the Vikings*, "it would be Scyld's distinction not that he had terrified some puny collection of peace-lovers but a people of whom the whole north stood in fear."[6] The poet was, then, saying something important at the start of his poem. It is not his fault if time and forgetfulness meant that he was not understood, by Anglo-Saxon scribes in 1000 CE or modern editors a thousand years later.

The Invention of the Scyldings

The poem goes on to say that Scyld Scefing was sent by God to save the Danes from being *aldorlease*, "without a lord." Legend outside *Beowulf*, but not inconsistent with it, says that he was washed up on shore as a foundling. He became a mighty king, and was succeeded by his son Beow, and his grandson Healf-dene, who was the father of Heorogar and Hrothgar and Halga, and perhaps of a daughter as well. When Scyld died the Danes returned him to the sea, in a ship packed with treasure—which, however, they did not set on fire in the traditional image of a "Viking funeral." They just let the sea take him, and the poet

---

5 Jordanes, *Origin and Deeds of the Goths*, trans. Charles C. Mierow (Princeton: Princeton University Press, 1908), reports on their height and on their expulsion by the Danes, chap. 3 (trans. Mierow, 23), and Procopius, *History of the Wars*, trans. H. B. Dewing, 7 vols., Loeb Classical Library (Cambridge, MA: Harvard University Press, 1914–40), bk. 2, chap. 25 (ed. Dewing, 1:487), on their fighting unarmoured, bk. 6, chap. 14 (ed. Dewing, 3:404–5), on killing their elderly males, and bk. 6, chap. 15 (ed. Dewing 3:415) on their resettlement by the Danes.

6 Gwyn Jones, *A History of the Vikings* (London: Oxford University Press, 1968), 29.

says, with obvious truth, "men can't say for sure, hall-councillors, heroes under the sky, who received that cargo" (lines 50b–52). The implication is, he and the treasure would go to the mysterious servants of God who sent Scyld as a foundling in the first place. But pushing an unguarded load of treasure out to sea seems highly dubious as a real-world practice.

Much of this, but not all, is corroborated by Danish legend, in many forms, and known collectively as "the legend of Lejre."[7] Some of it makes sense. The Danes being without a lord implies an interregnum, and something mentioned twice in the poem is the deposition of the Danish king Heremod, who gets a very bad write-up as a bloodthirsty tyrant, driven into exile. Being a bloodthirsty tyrant was not entirely a bad recommendation in the heroic world, and Heremod seems to have at least made an impression. In *Beowulf* he is compared to Sigemund, and in the Old Norse poem *Eiriksmál* Hermoth and Sigmund are the two favoured champions of Odin, who have the nerve to ask him why he is allowing the upstart Eirik Bloodaxe into Valhalla (the clue is in Eirik's nickname). Hermoth is also the hero chosen by Odin to ride down to Hel to demand the release of Baldur, a job which clearly requires a super-hero.

It seems likely, as far as *Beowulf* is concerned, that the deposition of Heremod and his exile to Jutland caused the initial interregnum. Did Scyld the mysterious foundling fill the gap? Or was it perhaps Healfdene, with the interesting name "Half-Dane," who then had one of his well-wishers compose for him a suitably glorious ancestry? Tolkien at least thought there never was anyone called Scyld—he had been invented as an ancestor by the "Shieldings," "the people of the shield," just like the Helmings, "the people of the helmet."[8] As for the word *Scefing*—is it a nickname? is it a patronymic?—all one can say is that someone whose father is called *Scef*, "Sheaf"

---

7 The relevant documents are conveniently collected and translated by Marijane Osborn, "Legends of Lejre, Home of Kings," in *Beowulf and Lejre*, ed. Niles and Osborn, 235–54.

8 Tolkien, *Beowulf: A Translation and Commentary*, 137.

(but how would anyone know what his father was called, if he was washed up on shore as a baby?); or who alternatively has a sheaf as his emblem, and whose son is called *Beow*, which means "Barley" (the manuscript reads *Beowulf*, but that is clearly a case of scribe A "jumping the gun"): well, he looks like someone out of a myth, framed by fertility-symbols.

With Healfdene, however, a bit of light dawns. But before considering him, it is worth considering what may have caused the whole process of roll-up, take-over, smashed halls, and dynastic change. The short answer is, the long shadow of the Roman Empire.

The Dark Ages: A Forbidden Topic

Modern historians do not like the term "Dark Ages" for the post-Roman centuries. Oxford University Press has even banned its authors from using the phrase, presumably because it seems disrespectful. There are two good reasons for keeping it, however. One is that it's dark to us. We know very little about the post-Roman period in western Europe: one of the first casualties of the failure of empire was widespread literacy.

The other is that it must have felt pretty dark for many people, as the result of—to quote Professor Ward-Perkins of Oxford's book *The Fall of Rome*—"a startling decline in western standards of living during the fifth to seventh centuries."[9] Many voices will be raised immediately, pointing for instance to the discoveries at Sutton Hoo, and saying, "how can you say such a thing? Look at all that lovely jewellery!" Ward-Perkins's point, however, is that civilization does not depend on an ability to produce aristocratic luxury items, but on low-cost, high-utility items like pots, tiles, nails, and, of course, coins—all of them familiar in the Roman world but scarce, poor-quality, or non-existent in places like Britain for centuries after.

9 Bryan Ward-Perkins, *The Fall of Rome and the End of Civilization* (Oxford: Oxford University Press, 2005), 87.

When did Rome fall? Answers vary, many insisting that it never fell at all—which, Ward-Perkins says, is why he wrote his book—but Rome was sacked by the Goths in 410, and in the same year the Romans evacuated Britain, which gives 410 a good claim to being the fatal moment.

What, however, was the effect on Scandinavia? Remembering always that one person's misfortune may well be another's opportunity.

The peoples beyond the Empire remembered the Dark Age also as a Heroic Age, the time of the great Gothic kings Ermanaric (died ca. 376) and Theodoric (the Goth, not the Frank called after him, died 526), as also the Burgundian kings Gibica and Gundahari, who would eventually be famed as the Nibelungs, the Lombards Alboin and Audoin, and not forgetting Hildebrand the old master-at-arms, who (according to another very old poem in Old High German) killed his own son in a duel between two armies. The Scyldings of *Beowulf* were absorbed into this corpus of legend as well, if at a somewhat junior level.

But what was *really* going on in Denmark, and when? Were they as badly affected as the unfortunate inhabitants of Britain in what is, to us, "the age of King Arthur"?

Dates are certainly unreliable, apart from the vital case of Hygelac (died ca. 530). But if we accept that Hygelac is still alive at the opening of *Beowulf* (clear enough), and if we accept (much more doubtfully) that Danish King Hrothgar is at that time very old, and is moreover the great-grandson of Scyld, then the Scylding ascendancy—the time of "taking away the mead-settles"—must be in the decades around the year 400, close to the fatal year 410.

It is absolutely certain that south Scandinavia in 400 was already a theatre of war, and had been, off and on, for centuries. Several archeological discoveries—at Hjortspring on the island of Als in south Denmark, at Nydam on Jutland close by, at Illerup in north Jutland—record occasions when raiding parties were cut off and overwhelmed by local defence forces: they involved, at Hjortspring, four boats, at this date (ca. 350 BCE) no more than paddled war-canoes, with a complement of ninety to one hundred men; at Nydam, with several depositions approximately 200–475 CE, several boats, quite like Viking boats but not as good, and in the last deposition more than a thousand items of weaponry including thirty-six swords; and at Illerup Ådal, several depositions again from a similar period, with one of them apparently the remains of a thousand-man army from Norway.[10] In addition, in several places in south Denmark there are further very large "weapon-dumps," where many weapons have been found, as at the three sites above mostly broken or made unusable, seemingly as sacrifice to the gods. Raiding each other, one may think, was what Scandinavians did.

The fall of empire, however, must have had knock-on effects to upset the old patterns of behaviour. People who had been doing well out of trade in amber and other luxury goods must have found they had lost their customers. Young men who might once have found employment as Roman auxiliaries no longer had this option. At the same time, there are many finds of gold in Denmark, and in southern Scandinavia more generally, but these are no longer buried with the dead (new men don't need ancestors?), instead are offered to the gods (in dangerous times, it's good to hedge one's bets?).[11]

Some people, in short, were doing well out of the post-imperial instability, but probably not the same people who had been doing well before. Professor Neil Price (once again of Uppsala University) suggests that what grew up post-400 was "a kind of gangster culture." Professor Hedeager, of Oslo,

---

10 See for the three sites mentioned, respectively Flemmin Kaul, "The Hjortspring Find: The Oldest of the Large Nordic War-Booty Sacrifices," in *The Spoils of Victory: The North in the Shadow of the Roman Empire*, ed. Lars Jørgensen, Birger Storgaard, and Lone Gebauer Thomsen, (Copenhagen: Nationalmuseet, 2003), 212–23; Erik Jørgensen and Peter Vang Petersen, "Nydam Bog—New Finds and Observations," in *The Spoils of Victory*, ed. Jørgensen et al., 258–85; Jørgen Ilkjær, *Illerup Ådal—Archaeology as a Magic Mirror* (Aarhus: Moesgård Museum, 2002).

11 Hedeager, *Iron-Age Societies*, 26n and figure 1.4.

argues that wars were no longer just a matter of raiding, but were fought to gain "territorial subordination"—much the same as "taking away the mead-settles," only in modern academic language.[12] Or, one might say, the gang-leaders trying to eliminate competition.

Summing up once more, in the first few lines of the poem the poet is describing what could be called the early stages of a process of state-formation, which would lead in the far future to the Kingdom of Denmark. The process of hall-destruction as described by Professor Herschend is also well described by Professor Näsman, who considers "the ethnogenesis of Denmark" from a different but complementary angle. In his view, the period 200–500 in southern Scandinavia was one of tribal warfare, with forty-seven recognizable spoils-of-war sacrifices at twenty-eight sites. What this meant, however, was that "the many polities were forced to join larger confederations through the pressure of endemic warfare." As a result: "In the archaeological record, the indicators of war seem to disappear after AD 500, not to reappear in large numbers till the Viking Age"—thus creating, for Denmark at least, a "Pax Danorum," a "Danish Peace."[13]

Translating Professor Näsman into Beowulfian terms, from the Roman period on, small Germanic tribes (like the Helmings and the Wylfings and the Brondings) were pressurized by outside forces (like the Huns and the Romans), and by internal competition (taking away the mead-settles) into combining into larger units, tribal confederations, which often became dominated by one tribe (in this case, the Scyldings). In this case also, the new tribal confederation must have acquired the name of "the Danes"—which seems to have meant originally something like, "the Flatlanders." (Most of Denmark is indeed notoriously flat. As the inhabitants of mountainous Norway often point out sarcastically, the Danes call a 482-foot hillock in Jutland *Himmelbjerget*, "Sky Moun-

12 Price, *The Children of Ash and Elm*, 73, Hedeager, *Iron-Age Societies*, 230.

13 Näsman, "The Ethnogenesis of the Danes," 5 (both quotations).

tain.") It does sound as if the name was given to the new Scylding-controlled confederation by its Scandinavian neighbours, perhaps rather derisively: people often accept rude names for themselves, like "Yankee," and turn them into a point of pride.

Leaving that supposition aside, the process just described also deals with a point raised by Professor Woolf, of St. Andrews, who warns that those who are fool enough to take *Beowulf* seriously as history should reflect that "much of the action might seem to take place before there were any Danes."[14] No, it takes place while the Helmings and other groups under the Scylding hegemony are learning *to call themselves "Danes"* and before news of the name-change and the political reorganization behind it has seeped out to the literate societies far to the south.

Näsman also points out that this "rapid social transformation" may have come about by both "military and political means" (conquest and dynastic marriage); while in his opinion, "the silent archaeological record" indicates that by about 500—the period just before the first scenes of *Beowulf*, when King Hygelac is still in his prime—"the Danes had won almost total hegemony in the eastern North Sea basin and the southwestern Baltic," putting a stop to the previously endemic inter-tribal warfare, of which there are so many earlier indications (like the smashed halls).

One further point made by Näsman, and again readily relatable to *Beowulf* (see p. 36 below), is that the new centralization extended also to religious practice. The offerings which used to be thrown into lakes and bogs now, ca. 500, start to appear "in settlement contexts" and even "in the postholes of the great halls of the magnates"—like Heorot.[15] The victorious elites had taken over religion as well as politics.

---

14 Alex Woolf, "Imagining English Origins," *Quaestio Insularis* 18 (2017): 1–20 at 18.

15 Näsman, "The Ethnogenesis of the Danes," 5, except "postholes," 7.

Such, then, is the background of Half-Dane son of Barley son of Shield son of Sheaf: an unlikely pedigree if ever there was one, but belonging to a man who was the heir to conquest, supplanter of the dynasty of Heremod, and the first non-mythical king of the Scylding line, resident by strongly-established tradition at what is now Lejre, not far from Copenhagen: a place of great discoveries.

Chapter 2

Old Legend, New Reality

The Archaeology of Lejre

With Healfdene *Beowulf* comes into contact with what is in effect the Danish myth of national origin, parts of which are told in at least eleven Scandinavian documents,[1] the longest and most complete accounts being that of Saxo Grammaticus, who wrote his *Gesta Danorum* in Latin ca. 1200, and the *Saga of Hrolf Kraki*, written in Old Icelandic ca. 1400—both of them hundreds of years later than any possible date for *Beowulf*. Other texts in the tradition include king-lists, Latin chronicles, and a Latin summary of the lost *Saga of the Skjöldungs* (that is, the Scyldings).

It has to be said right away that these are incredibly confused and contradictory.[2] Nevertheless there is one point where the whole Scandinavian tradition, the "legend of Lejre," is in solid agreement. Many texts declare that the power-centre of the Danish Skjöldung kings, the *Scyldingas* of *Beowulf*, was a place called *Hleiðargarðr*, or *Lethra*, or *Hledro*, or one of a number of other spellings: and this was early iden-

---

1 For which see again Osborn, "Legends of Lejre."

2 As discussed in Tom Shippey, "*Hrólfs saga kraka* and the Legend of Lejre," in *Making History: Studies in the Fornaldarsögur*, ed. Martin Arnold and Alison Finlay (London: Viking Society for Northern Research, 2010), 17–32; available at http://www.vsnrweb-publications.org.uk/fornaldarsogur.pdf.

tified as the village of Gammel Lejre, "Old Lejre," about thirty miles west of Copenhagen.

Till recently—just like the historicity of *Beowulf*—the tale was regularly dismissed as mere legend, Lejre being in modern times not much more than a hamlet. Hilda Ellis Davidson, editing the modern translation of Saxo, remarked that "there is no reason to suppose" Lejre was of any importance at the time the Skjöldungs were supposed to have lived, while Gwyn Jones's *History of the Vikings*, discussing the site, says regretfully, "It is sad to think of those high lords without a roof to their heads, but in respect of Lejre that is the case, and likely to remain so."[3]

Jones and Davidson guessed wrong. In the late 1980s the Lejre site was re-investigated, and to their considerable surprise the archaeologists have since found the remains of not one but a number of massive halls, built and rebuilt and inhabited for five or more centuries in succession from about 500 CE, and surrounded by other smaller buildings. No account we have space for here can do justice to the complexity of the successive discoveries, unfolded in a series of reports by Professor Tom Christensen,[4] but in brief, the first site to be explored, at what is now Mysselhøjgaard, revealed an enormous hall, 48.5 metres long, which was demolished and rebuilt on the same site three times between the late seventh and the late ninth century.

More relevantly for *Beowulf*, and not discovered till 2000, there was another and earlier hall at the site now called Fred-

---

3 Respectively Saxo Grammaticus, *History of the Danes*, trans. Peter Fisher, ed. Hilda Ellis Davidson, 2 vols. (Cambridge: D. S. Brewer, 1979), 2:46, and Jones, *History of the Vikings*, 47.

4 Christensen, "Lejre: Fact and Fable"; Christensen, "A New Round of Excavations at Lejre (to 2005)," trans. Faith Ingwersen, in *Beowulf and Lejre*, ed. Niles and Osborn, 109–26; and Christensen, "Lejre beyond the Legend: The Archaeological Evidence," *Settlement and Coastal Research in the Southern North Sea Area* 33 (2010): 237–54. The latest and most complete write-up is Christensen, *Lejre bag myten* [Lejre beyond the Myth] (Roskilde: Roskilde Museum, 2016), currently only available in Danish.

shøj. This hall, only slightly smaller at 45 metres by 7, was first built in the early sixth century, and remained in use until about 650, when it was demolished and apparently replaced by the hall at Mysselhøjgaard, about 500 metres to the south. Ownership of the whole Lejre site seems to have been continuous, as for one thing (Professor Christensen notes), when the 45 metre hall at Fredshøj was demolished in the first half of the seventh century, "an almost identical building was erected at Mysselhøjgaard," as well as the larger hall already mentioned. Christensen suggests "Perhaps this, and not the great hall at Lejre, was the most important building as far as Mysselhøjgaard was concerned."[5]

Be that as it may—and one has to note ruefully that archaeology can tell us what, but not often tell us why—the relationship between archaeology and poem is very obvious. *Beowulf* declares that King Hrothgar decided to build a hall "larger than the children of men had ever heard of" (69–70), and that is just what the archaeologists have so repeatedly found. The second or seventh-century hall at Mysselhøjgaard was described by Professor Christensen in 1991 as "the largest we yet know of from the Late Germanic Iron Age and the Viking period," while the earliest of the halls, at Fredshøj, nevertheless "must be classed among the very largest buildings known from the sixth century in Denmark."[6]

Nor is that the end of it, for in 2009 report came in of yet *another* series of excavations at Lejre, which unearthed two or perhaps three more halls built successively on another nearby site, the largest of them even bigger than anything previously discovered, almost 200 feet long by forty wide. It is the replica of this 60-metre hall which comes up if you google "King's Hall Lejre." The website's claim that "here the legendary hero Beowulf fought against the monster Grendel to defend the king's royal hall" has to be regretfully dismissed as just PR (this particular hall is too late), but there is

---

5 Christensen, "Lejre beyond the Legend," 250.

6 Respectively Christensen, "Lejre: Fact and Fable," 73, and Christensen, "A New Round of Excavations at Lejre," 122.

at least no doubt that the medieval legends had *some* basis in reality, and moreover that Lejre was an important site dating from the period already identified as that of the events in the poem, the early sixth century.

Not so long ago, who would have thought it?

Heorot and the "Harrow"

Lejre was, then, for centuries a centre of political power, but was it also—in line with Professor Näsman's remarks, see p. 30 above—something more? Long after his 1936 lecture,Tolkien developed a theory about this which has remained little-known and for which he had (at the time, as far as we can tell) little or no evidence. This was that Heorot was important because it was a sacred site, dedicated to the worship of Frey, known in Old Norse as Yngvi-Freyr, and (consistent with names like Sheaf and Barley) a fertility-god. In his incomplete "Commentary" on the poem, reworked and revised over many years and not published till 2014, Tolkien pointed out that in *Beowulf* Hrothgar is known as *eodor Ingwina*, "lord of the friends of Ing," and that he called his daughter Freawaru, "pledge of Frey"—though Frey-names are in Old English otherwise all but unknown.[7]

Tolkien does not mention the fact, and perhaps did not know of it, but his theory does in fact agree with the first report we have of Lejre, from the chronicler Thietmar of Merseburg. Writing in 1016, Thietmar said that Lejre (*Lederun*) in Sjælland (*Selun*) was the capital of Denmark, and that there human and animal sacrifices took place every nine years.[8] This may be part of the anti-Danish atrocity-narrative of southern chroniclers, but once again recent archaeology on the Lejre site has found evidence for it.

At both the main hall-sites of Lejre, the archaeologists discovered a heap of stones, marked by fire, with round them

---

7 Tolkien, *Beowulf: A Translation and Commentary*, 157, 179.

8 Osborn, "Some Medieval Sources for the Legendary History of Lejre," in *Beowulf and Lejre*, ed. Niles and Osborn, 297–99.

pits of animal bones. They concluded that these were sacrificial sites, and pointed to the description of what is called a *hörg* in the Old Norse poem *Hyndluljoð*:

> He's made an altar for me, heaped up with stones;
> Now that rubble has turned to glass;
> He's reddened it anew with the blood of kine.

This seems to confirm what Thietmar said, Professor Christensen concluding that "it seems natural...to interpret this part of the settlement area as the place where pagan acts of sacrifice took place."[9]

Tolkien of course did not know that (though he would have been fascinated to hear of it), but he was struck by what we can now see is a curiously similar report in *Beowulf*. Here the poet—in spite of his generally pro-Danish attitude—admits that under the stress of Grendel's attacks, the Danes did indeed resort to pagan idol-worship, *æt hærgtrafum* (line 175). *Hærg* is a rare word in Old English—it survives in the modern place-name Harrow—and scribe A in fact did not understand it, and wrote *hrærg* instead (which is meaningless). Nevertheless *hærg* is the same word as *hörg*, while *træf* means "tent"—and the name *Hleiðrar* itself is thought to mean "the place of the tents." So the Danes of *Beowulf* were worshipping idols at the "harrow-tents"? Or at the *hörg*, the altar, of *Hleiðrar*, "the tents"? (One might suggest, "tents" meaning the temporary encampments put up for the worshippers at Thietmar's winter sacrifice.)

There is just one more point to add in favour of the Heorot/Lejre connection. It is an inconvenient fact that Heorot is known only in English tradition, Lejre only in Danish tradtion. Nevertheless it's been noted—and by none other than Professor Niles, quoted already as a leading sceptic as regards the historical value of *Beowulf*—that in modern Lejre there is in fact a stream-valley, now usually dry except for seasonal flooding, but once probably a source of water for the great halls: and this is called Hjorterende, from Danish *hjorte* =

---

9 Christensen, "Lejre beyond the Legend," 252.

"stag," exactly like Old English *heorot* = "stag." There is no evidence that this is an ancient name, but no reason to think it isn't. Professor Niles remarks in non-committal fashion that the two names form "an intriguing onomastic coincidence."[10] Another of them. Just like the *hörg*, the *hærg*, and the tents.

There is anyway no doubt now that Lejre was a power-centre for many centuries, and from the start of the sixth century, if no earlier; and also probably a centre for pagan religion and pagan sacrifice. But does this cast any light on the Danish myth of national origin, also known as "the legend of Lejre," and on the way this is reflected in *Beowulf*?

The Legend of Lejre, Part I: Ingeld and Froda

As said above (before we got on to the real-life discoveries at Lejre), "the legend of Lejre" appears in at least eleven Scandinavian accounts, which are remarkably confused and contradictory.[11] There is nevertheless a general agreement that the start if it all was that Halvdan (i.e., Healfdene) was at odds with someone called Frothi (in *Beowulf*, Froda).

After that the various Scandinavian accounts all contradict each other. Saxo says that Haldanus kills Frothi, while the *Hrolfs saga* says it was the other way round. The saga says they were brothers, but Saxo says Frothi was Haldanus's father. The Latin *Lejre Chronicle* says that Haldanus was the son of someone called Ro, but the man who translated the chronicle into Old Danish, although he had an authoritative Latin text in front of him, was aware enough of a different version to challenge it, writing that Haldan had two sons, "and one was called Ro—but some say he was called Haldan—and the other was called Helgi."[12]

It's a pleasure to say that the author of *Beowulf*, in his allusive and indirect way, offers (if you can pick it out) a much

---

10 Niles, "*Beowulf* and Lejre," 190.

11 In addition to Shippey, "*Hrólfs saga kraka*," see Osborn, "Legends of Lejre."

12 Shippey, "*Hrólfs saga kraka*," 26.

clearer story than any of the Scandinavian accounts, which is not surprising, given that it is much earlier than most if not all of them. In one important point, moreover, *Beowulf* tells us something about the last stages of "the legend of Lejre" which seems to have been "airbrushed" out of Danish tradition altogether as disgraceful, even if horribly plausible: see pages 50–51 below.

Scribe A of the poem, however, seems to have done some airbrushing of his own, right at the start of the story. Having introduced Healfdene, with his suspect pedigree, he says (lines 57b–63):

> while he lived, he ruled, old and fierce in battle, the fortunate Scyldings. To him four children, all told, woke into the world, leaders of warbands, Heorogar and Hrothgar and Halga the good. I heard that the queen of ela, the consort of the warlike Scylfing.

There is no gap in the manuscript, but once again something has gone wrong. We're told there were four children, but we only get three names, plus "ela," which doesn't look like a name at all. Moreover, there is no verb after "I heard that"— so what was it that the poet heard? "Consort" and "queen" seems to be variants of each other, but where is the variant on "warlike Scylfing"? Also, the words as found in the manuscript do not carry alliteration and do not form a complete line.

The Scylfings are the kings of the Swedes, and one of them was called, elsewhere in *Beowulf*, Onela, so *some* child of Healfdene could have been married to him. Scholars have accordingly plucked from the confused Scandinavian traditions the name Yrsa, and filled it in, so line 62 now reads: "I heard that (Yrsa was) the queen of (On)ela, consort of the warlike Scylfing."

This gives us a complete line, and also makes sense, but why not say so? Because (and this is one other thing that Scandinavian tradition is agreed on) she was both wife and daughter of Helgi, or in *Beowulf*, Halga: her marriage was incestuous. The monastic scribe of *Beowulf* probably knew the story, but (here and elsewhere) he was not going to give any space to incest. Scrubbing "Yrsa" out of the poem leaves us with "Heorogar and Hrothgar and Halga the good" as the children of Heafdene—one wonders whether the poet perhaps thought that as "Yrsa" was both the granddaughter of Healfdene by blood, and his daughter-in-law by marriage, if you put the two relationships together she might be counted as a daughter and so as his fourth child? Heorogar the first son has however disappeared entirely from Scandinavian tradition (airbrushed out, see again pages 50–51 below), leaving Hrothgar (in Old Norse Hroarr), and Halga (in Old Norse Helgi).

Going back to the Frothi / Froda issue, *Beowulf* (in contrast to all the later Scandinavian stories) does not see him and Healfdene as relatives of any kind. Healfdene was king of the Danes, Froda was king of the Heathobeards (the "battle-beards"?). They were just enemies, which needed no explanation in a Heroic Age, but whoever killed whom in the first place, the Bards (as I call them) were not to be swept away or assimilated like smaller groups. But who were they?

It has to be said that the Bards are the most mysterious or at any rate under-reported group in the poem. Danes and Swedes, Jutes and Frisians, and even Geats, can be placed on the map, but the Bards have defeated researchers. One suggestion is that they may have been based in what was once called Bardengau, a district on the southern shore of the Baltic, around Luneburg Heath, where the German surrender was signed in 1945. But that seems too far away for a clash with Danes from eastern Sjælland, especially as the clash seems to have taken place early on in the Danish expansion and drive to the west.

Tolkien at least had a theory, which was: that the Bards were related to the Langobeards, or Lombards, who eventually settled in Lombardy. They were the stay-at-homes of a powerful group. They were moreover the original inhabitants of Sjælland, and the original owners of the site that became Heorot (or Lejre). They clashed with the incoming Danes as soon as the latter began their movement out of Skåne into Sjælland. The clash was an especially important one because it was about ownership of the sacred site at Lejre, and in *Beowulf* at least, it seems to have been decided—whatever Scandinavian accounts may say—by the killing of Froda the

Heathobeard by Healfdene King of the Danes, who thus became (in Tolkien's view) lord of Heorot.[13]

Something was, however, going to go wrong, and badly wrong, at Heorot. As soon as Heorot is completed in *Beowulf*, very near the start of the poem, the poet says, in his characteristically enigmatic way (lines 80b–85):

> the hall towered, high, wide-gabled. It waited for the surges of war, the hateful flame—it was not for a long time yet that the edge-hatred of son- and father-in-law (*aþumsweoran*) should reawaken after deadly enmity.

The poet does not say who the son- and father-in-law were, surely assuming that this and the fate of the hall were common knowledge to his original audience; and in fact he gets round to telling us at the right moment. When Beowulf gets back to his home in Geat-land, after killing Grendel and Grendel's mother, he rather naturally makes a report on the diplomatic situation in Denmark to his king and uncle Hygelac, and what he says is that Hrothgar, the Danish king, has decided to heal the old feud with the Heathobards by a diplomatic marriage, Hrothgar's daughter Freawaru to Froda's son Ingeld.

It won't work, says Beowulf. At the wedding, Beowulf speculates, some old Bardish veteran of the wars will point out to a young Bard the sword being worn by a young Dane. He'll say (Beowulf's own words, lines 2047–50), "Can you, my friend, *recognize* that sword, which your father carried to the battle…where the Danes killed him." In other words, "That's *your* sword, young fellow, look at him swaggering with it…" Then the fat will be in the fire, the Dane will be killed, the killer will get away, there goes the marriage and the alliance. (It's interesting to note that one explanation for the recently-discovered Staffordshire Hoard, which consists largely of disassembled sword-hilts, is that looted weapons were disassembled *just so they could not be recognized*: that was sure to cause future trouble.)[14]

---

13 See Tolkien, *Beowulf: A Translation and Commentary*, 331–33.

14 For the Hoard, see Chris Fern, Tania Dickinson, and Leslie Webster,

The deliberate irony is that, going by all other accounts, Beowulf got it wrong. He is of course prophesying, and what he prophesies is correct in outline but—as anyone in the original audience at all aware of heroic tradition would know, and surely most of them would—the truth was worse than Beowulf thought. It was not some nameless and unimportant young Heathobeard who would remember the old feud and take offence at the wedding, as Beowulf suggests. Instead it would be Froda's son Ingeld *himself* who would decide that he could not bear this alliance, and that it was his primary duty to avenge his father: a decision viewed by the northern world with great approval as the honourable thing to do (which explains the continuing popularity of the name).[15]

The disastrous marriage was accordingly a famous scene in legend. Another Old English poem, *Widsith*, a compendium of legendary names plus a few short vignettes, says briefly:

> Hrothulf and Hrothgar kept kinship together (*sibbe ætsomne*) for a long time, uncle and nephew (*suhtorgefæderan*), ever since they destroyed the race of the Wicings, beat down Ingeld's vanguard, cut down at Heorot the power of the Heathobeards.[16]

The Staffordshire Hoard: An Anglo-Saxon Treasure (London, Society of Antiquaries, 2019); for the theory, see Tom Shippey,"Place of the Slain," review of Fern et al., *The Staffordshire Hoard*, in *London Review of Books* 42, no. 5 (March 5, 2020): 33–34.

15 Tolkien did not agree, see *Beowulf: A Translation and Commentary*, 336–37. Here he remarks (twice) that the Norse version of the story, as found in Saxo book 6 (ed. Fisher and Davison, 1:175–95) is "brutalized," and that "an Ingeld, a profligate whose 'repentance' was shown by murdering his guests at his board, would not have beome the subject of English minstrelsy." He notes also that Ingeld and Freawaru both bear names with a Frey-element (Ing- and Frea-), and that such a love-story was "more likely really to arise in a people and family whose traditions are of Frey and Vanir rather than Odin" (338). See further p. 36 above.

16 *Widsith: A Study in Old English Heroic Legend*, ed. R. W. Chambers (1912; repr. New York: Russell and Russell, 1965), lines 45–49, with extensive notes on 205–6.

So the Bards were also the Wicings (cf. Helmings, Wylfings, Brondings). And according to this poem they were wiped out at Hrothgar's great hall of Heorot, at the wedding which didn't happen, and at a price: for though *Widsith*, note, says nothing about a wedding, it says there was a fight between Bards and Danes at Heorot. Meanwhile *Beowulf* says, very early in the poem, that Heorot was burned down in fighting between a father-in-law and a son-in-law. And who can these have been but Hrothgar, father of Freawaru the prospective bride, and Ingeld the prospective groom? So the fight, and the failed wedding, must have been at Heorot, and that was when the hall was burned down. We nowadays have to fit the bits of evidence together, but the poet seems to have assumed that to his original and knowledgeable audience, a hint would have been enough.

One has to concede that one disappointment as regards the archaeology of Lejre is that there is no sign of a burned-out hall (as hinted in *Beowulf*), nor of a major battle fought there much later on (as in the culminating scene of several Scandinavian accounts). One can only say that there is hope yet, for (as Professor Christensen points out) only a small proportion of the Lejre site has been excavated, and every new project brings something unexpected.

Nevertheless, summing up, at the time of Beowulf's visit to Heorot and his killing of Grendel the political situation in *Beowulf* looks like this. A hundred years before, the Scyldings, under their king Scyld (if he ever existed) had rolled up several smaller tribes, taken away their mead-halls, and incorporated them into the embryo Danish state. Later on, in the time of Healfdene, they ran into more determined opposition from the Bards, whoever and wherever they were. The ongoing feud between the ruling families is just about to be settled in favour of the Danes / Scyldings by their victory at the disastrous wedding. Hrothgar's diplomatic marriage plan isn't going to work, but just the same, on this front things are looking good for the Danes.

But what is the relationship between Hrothgar and Hrothulf, "uncle and nephew," as *Widsith* tells us, soon to be decisively victorious over Ingeld and the Bards?

The Legend of Lejre, Part 2: The Fears of Wealhtheow

Hrothulf is present in *Beowulf*, mentioned twice in the interlude between the first two fight sequences. In the poem, he never says anything and never does anything, and the poet never says who he is, but then he hardly needed to. Hrothulf is very clearly identifiable as Hrolf Kraki, the great Danish hero, their equivalent of his British contemporary King Arthur (but much better authenticated).

Before explaining his impassive, non-speaking, but vitally important role in the poem, one thing needs to be said: about national stereotypes. There is a general view (strongly held in France, and among the British elites) that Anglo-Saxons even now may be worthy fellows, but stolid, unsubtle—and, frankly, not too bright. Hint and allusion are lost on them.

This view is totally wrong. Anglo-Saxon poetry, and especially *Beowulf*, relies on hint and allusion, not to mention significant silence. Just like Tolkien (see p. 5 above) the poets liked to say things, very briefly, that were literally true, but had hidden meanings. Academic scholars, who love above all to say things at great length, with footnotes, do not relate well to this.

The pivotal figure for the major part of "the legend of Lejre" as presented in *Beowulf* is Hrothgar's queen Wealhtheow. Her name, incidentally, is regularly interpreted as meaning "foreign slave" (which puts her in her place), but this is probably another bungle by scribe A. It should be Wæltheow, or strictly speaking Wæl-theo, and mean "chosen servant" (of the gods), like Beowulf's father Ecg-theow, "servant of the edge or blade."[17]

She becomes prominent, like Hrothulf but more so, in the interlude between the killing of Grendel and the pursuit of Grendel's mother. In this the hall is cleared for a feast, rewards are given, a poet in Heorot sings a lay of Danish triumph, drink is being handed out, everything is fine.

---

17 As argued by Leonard Neidorf, "Wealhtheow and her Name," *Neophilologus* 102 (2018): 75–89.

Or is it? The poet goes straight on from saying, very approvingly, that "the mighty kinsmen, Hrothgar and Hrothulf took many a cup of mead in the high hall" (lines 1014-17a) to undercut the whole effect by adding, "Heorot was filled with friends; by no means did the Scylding-people at that time commit treacherous deeds" (lines 1017b-19).

Why say that (if everything is fine)? And what is the force of "at that time"? Does that mean they committed treacherous deeds some other time? And then (just after the song of triumph has been sung) Wealhtheow comes forward to "where the two good men sat, uncle and nephew" (*suhtergefæderan*, line 1164, exactly the same compound word as used in *Widsith*), and the poet once again adds ominously, and once again in words similar to those in *Widsith*: "at that time their kinship was together (*sib...ætgædere*), each was true to the other" (1164b-65a). Three times, then, twice in *Beowulf* and once in *Widsith*, a positive statement about Hrothgar and Hrothulf, uncle and nephew, is sharply qualified by adverbs of time: they kept peace together "for a long time," the Scyldings did not "at that time" commit treacherous deeds, the kinship of uncle and nephew was solid "at that time."

And immediately after the second set of rather ominous lines, Wealhtheow speaks. I give her speech (lines 1169-87) without comment, except to say that two hundred lines earlier, King Hrothgar had declared Beowulf his son, and told him he now had a "new family" (*niwe sibbe*). This is what she says:

> Take this cup, my lord, distributor of treasure. Be happy, gold-friend of men, and speak to the Geats with kind words, as a man must do. Be gracious to the Geats, think of gifts for them from what you have from far and near.
>
> Someone told me that you wished to have the warrior as your son. Heorot is cleansed, the bright ring-hall. Enjoy the rewards of many as long as you may, and leave folk and kingdom to your sons, when you must go forth and see destiny.
>
> I know my gracious Hrothulf, that he will hold the young ones in honour, if, friend of the Scyldings, you should leave the world before him. I expect that he will repay our sons

with good, if he remembers all the things we have done for
his pleasure and his honour during his childhood.

And then she goes and sits down by her own sons Hrethric
and Hrothmund—they have not been mentioned before—
where they sit among the *giogoð*, "the young ones." Beowulf
is sitting next to them.

It is surprising that this heavily-laden speech, which quite
changes the whole mood of the poem, was ignored for many
years of serious scholarship. Its significance was first pointed
out by a very junior scholar, whose name deserves to be
remembered, Ludvig Schröder, and he was not a top-flight
German professor but a Danish high school teacher, who had
read the poem only in Danish translation.[18] But he read the
poem without preconceptions.

Nobody took any notice of him, of course, until a top-
flight Danish professor backed him up, Axel Olrik. And then
the scholarly world refused to believe even him, especially
in England. Kenneth Sisam, another top-flight scholar from
Oxford, said you couldn't *possibly* draw any conclusions from
anything as indirect as this. The poem was written for warriors, men "not chosen for their intellectual ability," in fact
for dumb Anglo-Saxons if not dumb Englishmen (Sisam was a
New Zealander).[19] He assumed, like so many, that you could
be good at games or good at books but not good at both, or
to put it American-style, you could be a jock or a nerd. And
Beowulf was a poem for jocks. (Sisam, by the way, was Tolkien's tutor: they had a difficult relationship over the years.)

If one disregards the preconceptions, some things ought
to be clear from Wealhtheow's speech:

• she begins with a string of upbeat imperatives, and phrases
  complimentary to her husband.

---

18 See Shippey and Haarder, *Beowulf: The Critical Heritage*, 60–61,
372–73.

19 Kenneth Sisam, *The Structure of Beowulf* (Oxford: Clarendon,
1965), 9.

- but then she says, "Someone told me…" Is there a criticism there? "Why didn't you tell me, Hrothgar? Shouldn't I have had a say in this adoption?"

- much more clearly, note the switch from the imperative "enjoy" to the imperative "leave." Surely the "and" between them is really a "BUT," "give everything away by all means BUT NOT THE THRONE."

- it's also quite remarkable, and even more so in the original Old English, how Wealhtheow never says in so many words to Hrothgar, "once you're dead," though she says it in more indirect words three times, with a really rather beautiful use of the subjunctive or hypothetical mood, which it is impossible to capture in modern English. She even floats the idea that her husband may outlive his nephew, though since great stress has been placed on Hrothgar's age, that seems most unlikely.

- the gist of the first half of her speech is that she sees Beowulf, the stranger, who has just been adopted into his "new family," as a threat—and the threat is immediately revealed as a threat to her and Hrothgar's young sons, sitting, as we are carefully told, among the young ones, the *giogoð* as opposed to the *duguð*, the veterans. Adopting Beowulf sets him up as a competitor to them.

- and then she skips from Beowulf to Hrothulf. There is no obvious connection there. But there is a non-obvious connection, which is that Wealhtheow sees Beowulf as a threat, which he isn't, and her mind then jumps to Hrothulf as a threat, which he is.

Who, then, will be king of the Danes once Hrothgar is dead, which could happen any minute? The young sons of the king and queen, Hrethric and Hrothmund? Or the king's nephew Hrothulf, much older and already in a position of authority?

The situation hinted at in the poem is very similar to what happened in English history on the death of King Alfred the Great. Then (in 900) the kingdom passed to Alfred's son

Edward, but there was immediate rebellion from Alfred's elder brother's son Æthelwold, who in later centuries would have had the better claim. Æthelwold ran off and joined the Vikings, sparking a war between cousins.

Three Brothers, Four Cousins

One has to admire the artistic indirection with which the poet changes the whole mood of the poem, from a hall full of people celebrating the present to a woman desperately worried about the future—and trying to alter it, by placating one threat verbally (Hrothulf), and another by a magnificent gift, the gold neck-ring she presents to Beowulf. As she does so she asks him to be good to her sons, to be *dreamhealdende*, "a preserver of joy." Any Anglo-Saxon could have told her that *dream*, "joy," cannot be "held." It slips away.

Even the gift of the neck-ring does not fit the celebrations, for the poet says immediately, "Hygelac had that ring on his last journey" (lines 1202–3), only for it to be stripped from his dead body by the victorious Franks. So not even objects can be securely held, let alone happiness. There is something sad about Wealhtheow's last few words, which begin (lines 1228–29) as she looks round the hall), "Here every nobleman is true to the other, kind in heart, loyal to their lord..." That's right: for now.

But what happened next? And who is this person Hrothulf? The poet says he is Hrothgar's nephew, but does not say who his father and mother are. Fortunately, on this point Scandinavian tradition is once more rock-solid. Hrothulf, or in Old Norse Hrolf, is the son of Helgi (i.e., Halga) and Yrsa, the lady not-quite-identified in *Beowulf* as the queen of Onela (which she would be, perhaps, later in life, but see p. 62 below).

Hrolf's birth, however, is incestuous. According to *Hrolfs saga* (chap. 7 and following) Helgi raped a German princess, who gave birth to a daughter, whom she abandoned and to whom she gave a dog's name, Yrsa. The child was astonishingly beautiful, and years later Helgi saw her, carried her off—not knowing she was his daughter—and made her his wife.

She then gave birth to Hrolf, who is a child of incest: not that this was necessarily a bad thing for a hero, in some minds, for this meant that he was a true Scylding on both sides of his parentage. He then becomes, in all Scandinavian accounts, the first hero-king of the Danes.

Yes, but what happened to Wealhtheow's children? Do they appear in the Scandinavian accounts? Nothing is heard of Hrothmund in Scandinavia, and there is only one other Anglo-Saxon recorded as having the same name—the dates are not incompatible and they could be the same man, see p. 109 below. Is there a Scandinavian Hrethric? It would be odd if there wasn't. There would after all be no point in all these gloomy hints if there was not *some* follow-up story, which the poet might expect his audience—who knew all about the people-kings of the Spear-Danes, or so he tells us—to recognize.

Unfortunately, this time we don't know what the story was, but there are some unpleasant suggestions. The most direct of them comes from Saxo Grammaticus, who gives a long translation into flowery Latin of an old poem in Old Norse (we'd rather have the old poem). One line of this celebrates "Roluo" (i.e., Hrolf / Hrothulf) as the man *qui natum Bøki Røricum stravit avari*, "who laid low Røricus the son of the avaricious Bøkus." No-one has ever heard of Bøkus, it doesn't even look like a name, and it's suggested that Saxo misunderstood a phrase in Old Norse.[20] He saw something like *Hrœreks bani hnøggvanbauga*, "the bane of Hrœrek Ring-stingy," and thought it was not a nickname but a patronymic, something like *Hrœreks bani (sonar hins) hnøggva Baugs*, "bane of Hrœrek son of the stingy Baug," then Latinizing the names to Røricus and Bøkus.

Scandinavian tradition does moreover know of a king Hrœrek Hnøggvanbaugi, and the inference is that this was the Hrethric of *Beowulf*, who succeeded his father Hrothgar, but was killed by his cousin Hrothulf (Saxo's Roluo). One can only add that "ring-stingy" was not a good nickname for a

---

20 By Chambers, *Beowulf: An Introduction to the Study of the Poem*, 447.

Dark Age king to acquire. And it's interesting that the first piece of advice given by the poet of *Beowulf*, applying it to Scyld's son Beow) is, lines 20–25: "So shall a young man do good things, by splendid gifts while in his father's protection, so that the companions stay by him when he is older, help their lord when war comes: one thrives in every people through generous gifts." (Or, in very modern English, "everyone loves a bung.") Is this a comment on the story about to unfold? Or, just like Hrothgar's decision to build a very big hall, see p. 22 above, or Heorot and Hjorterende, see p. 38 above, it could be another coincidence.

All the above is inference, though very generally accepted (of course, as said at the beginning of this book, there are always those who follow the Sisam "too-clever-by-half" line, and say this is just "cherry-picking" from the horribly-confused Scandinavian sources). But there is one point where *Beowulf*, indirectly as always, offers a much better explanation of the Hrothulf / Hrolf story than anything from medieval Scandinavia.

This relates to the most famous event in King Hrolf's life, which is his death. In both Saxo and *Hrolfs saga*, what happens is that Hrolf is caught off-guard in his hall by attackers led by one Hiarvarthus / Hjörvarth, egged on by Skuld, a vaguely-supernatural creature, daughter of Helgi by an elfwoman. Neither Saxo nor the saga, however, have any idea who Hiarvarthus / Hjörvarth is. *Beowulf* does.

In Scandinavian tradition Healfdene / Halvdan has two sons. In *Beowulf* he has three, "Heorogar and Hrothgar and Halga the good." It is Heorogar who has vanished from Scandinavian memory. He never appears in *Beowulf*—at one point Hrothgar says sadly that he is dead already, "he was better than me." But he has a son, who is mentioned once in the poem. On his return to Hygelac, Beowulf tells his uncle (lines 2158–62) that among the gifts he received was the armour of Heorogar: Heorogar "did not wish to give it to his son, though he was loyal to him" (which is ominous in itself, inheriting family weapons being important in heroic culture). The son's name is Heoroweard, i.e., Hjörvarth.

In *Beowulf*, then, we have three brothers, not just two as in Scandinavian tradition, and four cousins: Hrothulf son of Halga, Hrethric and Hrothmund sons of Hrothgar, Heoroweard son of Heorogar. Conflating English and Scandinavian accounts, what happens is that the four cousins (except perhaps for Hrothmund) all kill each other. Hrolf kills Hrœrek Ring-stingy (Scandinavian tradition). Hjörvarth kills Hrolf (Scandinavian tradition, again, but only the English tradition sees the two men as cousins). Hjörvarth is then killed on the day of his victory, by the last loyal retainer of Hrolf. And that is the end of the House of the Scyldings.

A likely story? As mentioned above, civil war between cousins, and half-brothers, is a well-recorded feature of Anglo-Saxon history, and no doubt Dark Age history generally. One odd piece of corroboratory evidence is this. *Heoro*-names, apart from these two, are totally unknown elsewhere in Anglo-Saxon records—and we have a great many recorded Anglo-Saxon names. But there *is* such a name on an inscription, in runic letters, from Sweden, carved before the year 600: "hAeruwulafiz," or in Old English Heorowulf.[21]

So Heoro- names *were* known in Scandinavia at the time when these people were alive, in the early 500s, as they were *not* centuries later in Anglo-Saxon England. So the Anglo-Saxon poet couldn't have made the names up. They'd been *remembered*. And the critical figure is Heorogar, who has (in Scandinavian accounts) vanished completely from the Scylding family, so that a nasty civil war among relatives has become an unmotivated attack on the great hero-king by a complete stranger and an umpleasant witch-woman.

The story which is hanging round in the background of *Beowulf* sounds, frankly, a lot more plausible than the airbrushed accounts of Saxo and *Hrolfs saga*. It's not hard to see who would have benefited from the airbrushing.

---

21 Item 117 in Elmer H. Antonsen, *A Concise Grammar of the Older Runic Inscriptions* (Tübingen: Niemeyer, 1975), the Istaby Stone in Blekinge, Sweden. Professor Antonsen is in no doubt that the inscription represents what in Old English would be a Heoro-name.

Farewells and a Change of Focus

The last glance at the Scylding legend comes as Beowulf takes his leave of Hrothgar, to return home to Geatland, and it is another scene the point of which long escaped scholars (who, as commented already, are not good at hints and indirect statements, especially when these are being made with deliberate tact).

What happens is that first Beowulf says (lines 1818–39) that if he can help Hrothgar in any way in the future, he will. He goes on to say that if Hrothgar's neighbours threaten him, "as your enemies did formerly" (who does he mean?), then he will bring thousands of men to his assistance. He adds that he knows this will be ratified by Hygelac. And then he says that if young Hrethric would like to visit the Geatish court, he will find many friends there, closing with a proverbial remark: "far countries are better sought by someone himself worthy." This is polite on the surface—Beowulf is saying he is sure Hrethric is just the kind of worthy person to benefit from travel— but why say that now, and why put it proverbially?

Quite how to apply the proverb remains uncertain, but one important thing about giving advice by way of a proverb is that, in a sense, *you haven't said it*. You are only saying what people say. So the person you're talking to has to figure out how it applies, and no offence can be taken, because it's *impersonal*. Beowulf seems to be saying, however, that it might be a good idea to get Hrethric out of the country before his father dies and there's a struggle for succession: but, like Wealhtheow, he's not going to say that straight out.

In any case, Beowulf has not grasped the reality of his own situation, and readers of the poem, like the original audience, should have realized that: because the Hygelac disaster has already been mentioned. So Beowulf's confidence that he will have Hygelac's full backing in the future, along with unlimited resources, is completely mistaken.

Which Hrothgar indeed points out, for he replies, very politely (lines 1841–65) by saying first, that Beowulf is remarkably wise for one so young, as well as remarkably strong. But then, that if (1) Hygelac should be killed in battle, and (2)

Beowulf should survive, then (3) the Geats will have no-one better to choose as king, if (4) Beowulf is prepared to accept the throne. All of which happens, except that (as Hrothgar has guessed) Beowulf will *not* be prepared initially to accept the Geatish throne.

What the scene shows us, in fact, is two men, each of whom sees and points to the danger hanging over the other, while neither sees the danger hanging over himself: a scene of sad irony (very characteristic of the literature of the old North more generally).

But with that the focus shifts from Denmark to what is now Sweden—though it wasn't Sweden then.

Chapter 3

The Bigger Picture

A Long Vendetta

Beowulf goes home. He makes his report to Hygelac, including his gloomy prophecy about the planned Freawaru–Ingeld marriage. And then, with something of a clash of gears—it certainly fooled scribe B, who matches scribe A with another total misunderstanding of an important name—we are many years on, and Beowulf has been king of the Geats for fifty of them. In the meantime a great deal has happened.

One should say that no-one now believes in Beowulf's fifty-year reign: there is no corroboration of this, no mention of Beowulf anywhere in Scandinavian or for that matter English legend, everything to do with Beowulf is fiction, and so is the dragon which will kill him. The question is, whether the very detailed and extended account of the history of the Geats and Swedes which runs through the last third of the poem can be dismissed as readily as Dr. Gahrn would have it (see p. 2). It is not as strongly corroborated as Hrothgar and Hrothulf and events in Denmark, but it fits well with what legendary accounts we do have, and (once again) makes much better sense than they do.

Since the poem says nothing in chronological order, it is best at this stage to set out events as they can be fitted together. They look—remembering what Professor Price says about "gangster culture," see p. 28 above—like a prolonged vendetta between two ruling families.

This goes on over three generations. The royal dynasty of the Geats, in south Sweden, starts with a grandfather, Hrethel. He has three sons, Herebeald and Hæthcyn and Hygelac, and an unnamed daughter, who is the mother of Beowulf. Hygelac's son is Heardred, so Beowulf is his maternal cousin. The Swedish royal dynasty, from north Sweden, also has a grandfather, Ongentheow. He has two sons, Onela and Ohthere. Ohthere has two sons, Eanmund and Eadgils. Of these eleven named men, six Geats and five Swedes, five will die in the vendetta. As far as we know, none will suffer the shame of a natural death—unless grief counts as "natural causes." Briefly and chronologically:

- Herebeald is accidentally shot with a bow by his brother Hæthcyn: "he missed the mark and shot his kinsman, one brother the other with bloody dart," says the poem, line 2439. (An heir to the throne being shot by the next in line is always suspicious.)

- Their father Hrethel dies of grief.

- We do not know what causes the Swedish–Geatish vendetta (just being neighbours may be explanation enough in Heroic Age circumstances), but in what we might call the First Geatish–Swedish War, its first casualty is Hæthcyn, killed in battle by the Swedish grandfather Ongentheow.

- Ongentheow is killed himself the next day by Hygelac, coming to the rescue and arriving just too late.

- Hygelac is then killed raiding in the Netherlands.

- Beowulf is offered the throne, but (unlike Hrothulf, one might say) insists on passing it to his cousin Heardred.

- meanwhile Onela has succeeded to the Swedish throne, but his nephews Eanmund and Eadgils have rebelled against him and taken shelter with the Geats.

- Heardred decides to support the rebels, which is a bad mistake, for (in the Second Geatish–Swedish War) Onela pursues his nephews and kills both Heardred and his nephew Eanmund.

- Beowulf succeeds Heardred and kills Onela, thus avenging Heardred, apparently in a battle (famous in legend) fought on the ice of Lake Väner in central Sweden, this being the Third Geatish–Swedish War.

- Eadgils, the surviving son of Ohthere, becomes king of the Swedes, but if one expects gratitude from him, or his heirs, towards his Geatish allies, then one has not grasped Heroic Age realities. Once Beowulf is dead from dragon-bite, the poet assumes that whoever is king of the Swedes— whether this is still Eadgils or not—he will finish off the Geats as an independent power for good. (Which is why Gothenburg is now part of Sweden—in Swedish *Sverige*, derived from older *Svea-riki*, "kingdom of the Swedes"— instead of Stockholm being part of Gothland.)

How much of this can be corroborated or believed in?

The Geatish Kings: Long Forgotten, but Now We Know...

The first thing is that there is no corroboration anywhere of most of the Geatish dynasty, no mention anywhere of Hrethel or Herebeald or Hæthcyn or Heardred (but see further pp. 114–15 below)—or of Beowulf, as said already. One might as well say that according to the evidence there never was any Geatish dynasty—except for the fact that Hygelac is the only person in the poem who is quite definitely historical, and is remembered as a Geat not only in *Beowulf* but by the *Liber monstrorum*. If he is genuine, then maybe the others are too.

Hygelac is actually remembered in Scandinavian tradition, but in a way which suggests that nothing was remembered about him *except his name*, not even his undoubtedly historical death. He (or anyway his name) appears in "The Saga of the Ynglings," which forms the first part of the great compilation of kings' sagas written by the Icelander Snorri Sturluson sometime in the 1220s. That is long after *Beowulf*, but Snorri based his saga on a much older poem, which he frequently quotes, the *Ynglinga Tal* or "List of the Ynglings," which may have been written as early as 870—long before Snorri, but still probably not as old as *Beowulf*.[1]

What Snorri says about Hugleikr (= Hygelac) is in any case all but definitely wrong. He starts by saying that Hugleikr became "king of the Sviar," that is to say, the Swedes, and he "was no warrior," and goes on to allege that he was totally frivolous: "He had in his court a lot of all kinds of players, harpists and fiddlers."[2] Hygelac, however, is identified as king of the Geats in English tradition, and as king of the Danes by the Frankish chroniclers: neither early tradition makes him king of the Swedes, while the one certain fact about the historical Hygelac is that he *was* an aggressive warrior. As for the "harpists and fiddlers," it looks very much as if Snorri made the same mistake as several modern commentators. He knew nothing about Hugleikr except his name, construed the name as *hugr* = "mind" + *leikr* = "play" and decided it meant "the frivolous mind." Old Norse *leikr*, like Old English *lac*, does mean "play," but in names like Guth-lac, "war-play," or the phrases *ecga gelac*, *sweorda gelac*, it means "the play of edges / swords," in other words "battle." So Hygelac's name really meant "the warlike mind": much more the kind of name Heroic Age parents were likely to give their sons.

In Norse tradition, then, Hygelac had dwindled to being nothing but a name, and that misunderstood. Even less, in fact nothing, is known of his relatives as given in *Beowulf*. But one thing *Beowulf* makes very clear is that they were the losers. In whose interest was it to remember them?

---

1 See Snorri Sturluson, "Ynglinga Saga," in *Heimskringla*, trans. Alison Finlay and Anthony Faulkes, 2 vols. (London: Viking Society for Northern Research, 2011–2014), 1:6–47.

2 *Ynglinga saga*, chap. 22 (trans. Finlay and Faulkes, 24).

The Swedish Kings: Well-Remembered, but Now Not So Sure…

Beowulf's Swedish kings naturally, therefore, survived a little better. Ohthere, Onela, and Eadgils are all remembered in their Norse forms as, respectively, Ottar, Ali, and Athils, though the name of their father/grandfather Ongentheow is given by Snorri as Egil, not Angantyr as we might expect. As with the grandsons of Healfdene, however, the relationships between the Swedish kings have sometimes been lost; while over the centuries, what sticks in the collective memory is dramatic incidents, and of these there are two.

The first is the battle on the ice of Lake Väner, mentioned by Snorri,[3] hinted at by *Beowulf*, and further commemorated in an Old Norse poem, *Kálfsvísa*,[4] which gives a list of heroes and the horses they rode to the battle: Ali's horse was Hrafn, Athils's horse was a grey called Slungnir, and in this battle (all agree) Ali was killed. Snorri however does not recognize Ali as a Swede, and instead says he was from Uppland in Norway. But there is also an Uppland in Sweden.

In much the same way Snorri gives Ottar son of Egil the nickname "Vendil-crow," and says he was killed raiding Vendil in North Jutland (where the *Wendle* of *Beowulf* came from). Snorri further identifies Athils, the victor at the battle on the ice, as the son of Ottar, agreeing entirely with *Beowulf*, which gives Eadgils as son of Ohthere.[5] The battle between Onela/Ali and Eadgils/Athils was remembered identically, then, in England and in Scandinavia. What was forgotten in Scandinavia—just as with Hrothulf, Hrethric, and Heoroweard—was that this was a civil war, this time between uncle and nephew, not between cousins.

---

3 *Ynglinga saga*, chap. 28 (trans. Finlay and Faulkes, 32).

4 Three stanzas of the poem (there called *Alsvinnsmál*) are quoted by Snorri: see Snorri Sturluson, *Edda*, ed. and trans Anthony Faulkes (London: Dent, 1987), 136–37.

5 *Ynglinga saga*, chap. 27 (trans. Finlay and Faulkes, 30–31).

The close correspondence between *Beowulf* and Snorri looked conclusive to earlier scholars. A hundred years ago, indeed, R. W. Chambers, following the Swedish archaeologists Knut Stjerna and Birger Nerman, was quite sure that the burial mounds of three of the five prominent Scylfings mentioned in *Beowulf* had been securely identified.[6] Two of them were in Uppsala, where there are three mounds still generally agreed to be royal burials, just because of their size. Chambers's argument was that only three Swedish kings were said by Snorri, in the *Ynglinga Saga*, to have been "laid in mound" in Uppsala, and they were Aun the Old (who does not appear in *Beowulf*), his son Egil, and Egil's grandson Athils. (Athils = Eadgils.) His grandfather is named Egil by Snorri and Ongentheow by *Beowulf*, but (Chambers argued) they must be the same person.

But what of Ongentheow's two sons, Ali/Onela and Ottar/Ohthere? Particularly conclusive, for Chambers, was the existence of a mound called *Ottarshøgen* to the north of Uppsala, in the Vendel district. According to Snorri, King Ottar's nickname was *Vendilkráka*, "Vendil-crow," because he had been killed while raiding Vendil in North Jutland.[7] But (Chambers argued, repeating Birger Nerman) Snorri had got it wrong, just as he had with *Hugleikr*. Ottar must actually have been called "Vendel-crow," not because he died in Vendil, Jutland but because he was buried, against family custom, in Vendel, north Sweden: Snorri's Jutland story, like his frivolous-Hugleikr story, was pure invention. But *Ottarshögen* meant that we now had three mounds for Egil/Ongentheow, Athils/Eadgils, and Ottar/Ohthere—while the other great Scylfing king, Ali/Onela, had died in battle on Lake Väner, his body presumably not recovered.

Chambers further argued that the dates of the mounds could be squared with *Beowulf*: Aun's mound (the oldest) ca. 500, Egil/Ongentheow's mound about 510, i.e., well before

---

6 See Chambers, *Beowulf: An Introduction to the Study of the Poem*, 356–57, 408–18.

7 *Ynglinga saga*, chap. 27 (trans. Finlay and Faulkes, 30–31).

the Hygelac disaster, Ottar/Ohthere's about 525 (Chambers's date for the Hygelac disaster), and Athils/Eadgils's much later, 570–580. These dates were pretty much what the archaeologists of Sweden (at that time) also figured, QED.

It was and is a very attractive theory, but it has not stood the test of time. The Uppsala mounds are now reckoned all to be later than 550, too late for the *Beowulf* characters (apart from Athils/Eadgils). On the other hand, latest opinion on the mound in Vendel ("Ottar's mound") is that "the most probable dating of *Ottarshögen* is around AD 520–30,"[8] which would agree very well with *Beowulf*, for the poem implies that the death of Ohthere, the consequent rebellion of his sons against Onela, and the killing of Heardred, all took place shortly after the Hygelac disaster, conventionally dated 525–530. The trouble here is that it is now pretty certain that the name *Ottarshögen* is not an ancient survival at all: it was made up in the seventeenth century by a Swedish antiquarian—who had also read Snorri and knew about "Vendel-crows."[9] So we don't know who that mound was raised for, and there is no reason to think that it was for the King Ohthere of *Beowulf*. Another attractive theory slain by a brutal fact...

Allowing for many uncertainties, one has to conclude that the Scylfings of Sweden are not as readily located as once they were, or as the Scyldings of Denmark now are at Lejre.

---

8 For the Uppsala mounds, see John Ljungkvist, "Dating Two Royal Mounds of Old Uppsala," *Archaeologisches Korrespondenzblatt* 38, no. 2 (2008): 263–82 at 277, and for the Vendel mound, John Ljungkvist and Andreas Hennius, "The Dating of Ottarshögen and the Emergence of Monumental Burial Grounds in Middle Sweden," in *Re-Imagining Periphery: Archaeology and Text in Northern Europe from Iron Age to Viking and Early Medieval Periods*, ed. Charlotta Hilderdal and Kristin Ilves (Oxford: Oxbow, 2020), 91–101 at 98.

9 Ljungkvist, private communication. The research on this is forthcoming from Professor Daniel Sävborg.

What the Poet Had in His Head

The other dramatic incident involving the Scylfing kings, generally remembered, was the clash between Athils and Danish king Hrolf. According to *The Saga of Hrolf Kraki*, chs. 25–30, what happened was that Hrolf was urged to visit King Athils at his court in Uppsala, to recover his father Helgi's inheritance. Hrolf and his companions faced treacherous attacks and sorcery from Athils, but were guided by Odin and assisted by Hrolf's mother Yrsa, in the saga, married to Athils. In the end they collected a vast haul of treasure and rode off, hotly pursued by Athils and vengeful Swedes, but Hrolf cunningly dropped gold rings on the trail. The Swedes stopped to pick them up, and in the end even Athils bent from his horse to do so. At this point Hrolf, turning back, wounded Athils in the buttocks as he groped to recover a ring from the mud, and said, "Now I have bowed like a swine (*svinbeygða*) him who is greatest of the Swedes." Snorri uses the same word, *svinbeygða*, in his account of the same incident, in the "Poetic Diction" section of his "Prose Edda":[10] making Swedes grovel in the mud like pigs was, for Norwegian-descended Icelanders, the main point of the story.

This sounds very much like neighbourly Danish/Norwegian teasing of the Swedes (a practice not unknown even now), and *Beowulf* never mentions or alludes to it. But it does raise two issues, one major, one minor. The minor one is the apparent contradiction between what *Beowulf* does not quite say, namely that Hrolf's mother Yrsa became "the queen of (On)ela," see p. 39 above, and the Scandinavian view that she became the queen of Athils (or Eadgils), the son of Ali/Onela. Is it likely that a son would marry his father's widow? Actually, there is more than one parallel to this in recorded Anglo-Saxon history: when King Alfred's father Æthelwulf died in 868, his wife, the Frankish princess Judith, was promptly remarried to his son Æthelbald, and the same thing happened with King Æthelberht of Kent (died 616), his Frankish

---

10 *The Saga of King Hrolf Kraki*, trans. Byock, 67, Snorri Sturluson, *Edda*, trans. Faulkes, 112.

wife Bertha, and his son King Eadbald. One might conclude that diplomatic marriages were also political alliances, too important to be terminated by the death of one party. So the contradiction between sources is not irresolvable.

The major issue for *Beowulf*, however, is that the stories told in the poem about the Danes, and the Swedes, and the Geats (and even the Bards here and there) are *all inter-connected*. This, in fact, is a large part of what causes the "air of reality and truth" in *Beowulf* conceded even by sceptics like the modern Klaeber editors. The poet delivers a whole pile of information about the Scyldings, some corroborated, some not, but giving a much more plausible story than any other account. He also delivers a whole pile of information about the Swedes and the Geats, the Scylfings and the Hrethlings, most of this *not* corroborated, but again much better linked-up than any other account.

The sheer complexity of this is best indicated by the attached diagram. I do not suggest that readers should try to check this, or even try to trace it out, though it's all correct. Note nevertheless the careful *glissando* round the incestuous birth of Hrolf, and the fact that Heorogar's name, unlike almost all other characters, has no Norse equivalent. Note also that the "daughter of Healfdene" who marries Onela may (or may not) be the same as "Yrse" who marries Eadgils.

The point of the diagram is simply that all this is *what the poet had in his head*, which he conveyed in the poem without stress, emphasis, or comment. Indeed he did it sometimes so casually that it looks careless. He never tells us who Hrothulf is: we had to figure that out. Who Hygelac is slips out only, late on, by use of the phrase *Higelac Hrethling*. The poet never tells us who Beowulf's successor is, Wiglaf, and no satisfactory theory has ever been produced. And though Hnæf is identified as a Scylding (line 1069), we have no idea where he, or his sister Hildeburh and father Hoc, fit in on the family tree.

Nevertheless, the poet never contradicts himself, easy though that would be. Matters he does not explain—like the rebellion of Ohthere's sons against their uncle Onela—nevertheless find a ready explanation, see p. 70 below. As Tolkien points

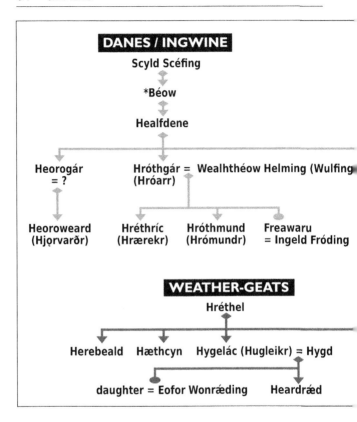

out—see again p. 70 below—matters which seem peculiar, even unlikely, make sense in the light of political manoueverings.

Along with all that, moreover, is the strange introduction, by the poet, of information which is quite unnecessary, and only makes matters more complex. A prize example comes as Wiglaf advances to help Beowulf as he is losing his fight with the dragon, when the poet stops the action to tell us where Wiglaf got his sword, in the strange historical flashback already mentioned, p. 16. The sword belonged, we are told, to the Swedish rebel Eanmund, whom Wiglaf's

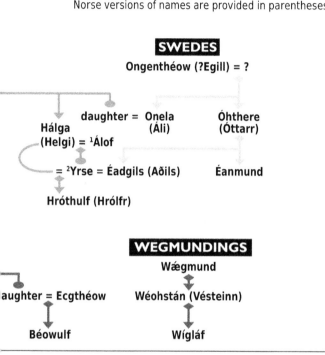

Figure 1. Genealogical table of lords and ladies in the world of Beowulf. By Sam Newton. Note that Old Norse versions of names are provided in parentheses.

father Weohstan killed in the battle where Beowulf's cousin Heardred also fell.

So Weohstan was *on the other side* from Beowulf? What is his son doing helping Beowulf, and indeed, why does Beowulf tolerate ownership and display of a sword used in the battle where his king and cousin Heardred was killed (just the kind of thing that causes trouble elsewhere in the poem, see pages 41 and 84)? Moreover, the poem is very clear that Wiglaf and Beowulf are closely related—the last thing Beowulf says to Wiglaf as he dies is, "You are the last of our race, the

Wægmundings." But the *first* thing we are told about Wiglaf is that he is a *leod Scylfinga*, "a man of the (Swedish) Scylfings." The only sensible explanation is that Beowulf's father Ecgtheow must have been a Swede as well, who went over to the Geats long ago, just as Wiglaf seems to have done. And what makes Beowulf a Wægmunding? His name doesn't begin with a W-, like Wiglaf and Weohstan, as you would expect.

None of this is impossible, but none of it helps the narrative at all, it only raises questions. Changing sides in civil wars is the kind of thing that happens in reality, but why *invent it* if it has no purpose in fiction? The simple explanation is that the poet (and his original audience) had already heard something of these stories, and they accepted it as fact. They may well have known about Weohstan, Wiglaf's father, for instance, for the poem about the battle on the ice has one Vestein riding to it: his horse was called Val. If he was the same man as Weohstan, who in *Beowulf* killed the rebel-nephew Eanmund in an earlier battle and passed Eanmund's sword on to his own son Wiglaf, then in the battle on the ice Vestein must once again have fought for King Ali / Onela: as indeed he seems to have done.[11] Some time later, however, Weohstan's son Wiglaf must have changed sides, from Swedes to Geats—like Ecgtheow many years before?

Modern Novel or Ancient Epic?

There are really only two possibilities here. One is that the poet was behaving like a modern novelist. He was trying to create what the critic Roland Barthes calls "the reality effect," which is, to quote Barthes, "the basis of that unavowed verisimilitude which forms the aesthetic of all the standard works

---

11 Nelson Goering comments (private communication) that Vestein's position at the start of stanza 2 groups him with the followers of Ali, on this occasion the losers, which agrees with the fact that *Beowulf* credits him with the killing of Eanmund, Onela/Ali's rebellious nephew, in an earlier battle (when Ali's men were the winners).

of modernity." This is done by loading the narrative with "useless details" of which (Barthes again) "every narrative, at least every Western narrative of the ordinary sort nowadays, possesses a certain number."[12] All novelists now know they have to do this. Describe what the characters see, describe their furniture, mention the weather, whatever, none of it necessarily *meaning* anything, or doing anything for the progress of the actual narrative. It's all there just to make the narrative *seem real*.

The *Beowulf*-poet could have been doing just that. Certainly the density of his family-trees, the casual way they are presented, and even the gaps in them here and there are exactly what create the "air of reality and truth" which the Klaeber editors grudgingly concede. But is that likely? Note Barthes' careful qualifications above: "modernity," "nowadays." The "aesthetic" he describes is strikingly anachronistic in an ancient epic. A much simpler solution is that the poet mentions all the details he does because he thought that, to his original audience, they were common knowledge: which would explain also why he does not bother to identify characters like Hrothulf, Hoc, Wiglaf. To that original audience the details were not "useless" at all: they *meant* something, even if we don't now know what.

There is a further semi-statistical argument, drawn from the seventy-odd names in the poem. Nearly half of these are mentioned once only—like Yrmenlaf, Grendel's victim's younger brother, or Heatholaf, said to have been killed by Beowulf's father—and rather more than half of them known only from *Beowulf*. If these were mostly inventions, made up to create "the reality effect," one would expect the "singletons"—easiest to invent and drop in—also to be the "unknowns," the ones who don't figure elsewhere in northern legend. But in fact there is no such correlation. Froda and

---

12 Roland Barthes, "The Reality Effect," in Barthes, *The Rustle of Language*, ed. François Wahl, trans. Richard Howard (Berkeley: University of California Press, 1989), 141–48 (148, modernity; 142, details, nowadays).

Eomer are mentioned only once, but both are well-recorded elsewhere, even famous. Conversely, people mentioned repeatedly and said with some force to be well-remembered, like Ecgtheow, have left no trace. No-one knows who Wiglaf was, prominent though he is at the end of the poem, but as said just above his father Weohstan, completely irrelevant within the poem, does crop up elsewhere. This random distribution cannot have been planned. It is what you would expect of someone drawing on a body of legendary / historical material, of which only a portion has purely by chance survived.[13]

The same goes, furthermore, for the surprising number of stories hinted at in the poem but never actually told—their number disguised for modern readers by the well-meant efforts of editors to fill the gaps. We think we know how Heorot came to be burned down (lines 82–85), thanks to five lines from *Widsith*. But what is the full story of Ecgtheow's exile and restoration (459–72)? What started the fight at Finnsburg, who was it between, what are the details of the Jutes' (alleged) bad faith, and what were the Jutes doing in Frisian Finnsburg anyway (1066–1159, and see pp. 85–87 below for a suggestion)? Going on (and for these questions there are no suggestions), why were the Danes and Geats on bad terms some time in the past (1855–58)? What did the Geats do to the Swedish king Ongentheow's wife—it seems to have annoyed him a great deal (2930–41)—and what did "Hemming's kinsman" Offa do to change the character of Queen Fremu, long thought to be Queen Modthrytho (1944–54)? What is the story of the Danish / Heathobeardan conflict, when Withergyld was killed (2047–52)—his name appears also in *Widsith* line 124, though without further details?

Closer to the poem's core, there is the whole issue of the Wægmundings, while perhaps most tantalizing of all is the tale of how Unferth, Hrothgar's counsellor, and under strong suspi-

---

13 The names in the poem are discussed in more detail in Tom Shippey, "Names in *Beowulf* and Anglo-Saxon England," in *The Dating of Beowulf*, ed. Neidorf (Woodbridge: Boydell & Brewer, 2014), 58–78.

cion of having a role in the Scylding civil war, killed his brothers. Beowulf accuses him of this (lines 587–89), and the accusation is confirmed by lines 1167–68. One wonders how a fratricide can continue to be held in honour in a heroic court, while recognizing that fights between family members are a standard part of the heroic repertoire—but we are left to speculate.

There are admittedly places where we think we know how to fill in the gap in a story, as in the case of the burning of Heorot, or the incest of "Yrsa" above. There has moreover long been a scholarly industry of explaining that, far from being "digressions," the poem's many allusions are doing important jobs in context, as indeed they often are: the contrast of Sigemund and Heremod (875–915) makes a point about heroic careers, the Finnsburg story (1066–1159) introduces a female perspective to the poem, and so on. But once again scholarly industry has tended to blur over the many occasions where we are left twisting in the wind—the list of "untold tales" just above is by no means complete.

Are we meant to think that the poet invented all these questions *just so they could not be answered*? Just to thicken up his invented background, and create the Barthesian "reality effect"? It seems a strangely anachronistic process for an ancient poet. But this is what must be meant by Tolkien's claim that none of this is history, it's all "literary art." It's a pity he never explained himself, and nor have his many followers. (But then, as we shall see, Tolkien didn't really mean it.)

The other option, as said above, is simpler. The poet spent so much time and effort on the background of his fairy-tale of troll, hag, and dragon, putting in all the names and allusions, because he thought, rightly or wrongly, that it was all true, all historical fact. He expected his original audience to recognize the names and understand the allusions—and check or challenge him if they disagreed with them—because they also thought it was true, part of their own history and heritage.

Putting it briefly, the poet knew what he was talking about. He knew more than we do. And, as we shall see, centuries later and across the sea in England, he may still have had strong motivation to remember.

No Dates, but a Sequence of Events

First one needs, once again, to consider, if not dates, then the sequence of events. According to the poem, after the death of his cousin Heardred Beowulf rules successfully, dominating all opposition for fifty years, which given that Heardred succeeded to the throne only after the death of his father ca. 530 takes us almost up to the end of the sixth century. No-one, however, believes this. As said twice already, everything connected with Beowulf personally looks like fiction, trolls, dragons, and swimming home from the Netherlands carrying close on a ton of salvaged armour.

Instead one has to note that after the Swedish king Ongentheow was killed by Hygelac at Ravenswood, he must have been succeeded immediately by one or other of his two sons—I give all names in this section their Old English rather than their Old Norse forms—Ohtere and Onela. If he was succeeded by Ohthere, and then, when Ohthere died, the throne was claimed by his brother Onela, then that on its own would be good motivation for the rebellion of Ohthere's sons Eanmund and Eadgils, excluded from the throne. When they sought support from their Geatish neighbours, however, they went to Heardred, so Hygelac must already have been dead, and the Geats—their king dead in the Netherlands with most or all of his top-rank warriors—must have been in a weak position: which is why Onela was able to kill both his rebellious nephew Eanmund and the young Geatish king Heardred. There is no hint known as to how long it took for the Geats and the remaining Swedish rebels to pull themselves together and defeat Onela on the ice of Lake Väner, except that Eadgils—the surviving son of Ottar—is seen in legend as a contemporary and enemy of Hrothulf, who is clearly set to take over Denmark at about the same time as the fall of Hygelac.

A further point, made by Tolkien, is that even casual allusions in the poem can be seen to fit the sequence above. Twice in the poem reference is made to earlier hostility between Danes and Geats, with the Danes sending gifts as tokens of good will. Tolkien remarks that the moment for this "policy of appeasement" appears to fit Hrothgar's character—he is just about to try something similar with Ingeld and the Heathobeards—and the moment for it would clearly be "after the disastrous death of the old Swedish king Ongentheow and the accession of Hrethel's third and very warlike and ambitious son Hygelac."

But isn't it strange that when Beowulf arrives at Hrothgar's court, he is visiting a king whose niece/ex-daughter-in-law, i.e., the mysterious "Yrsa," is "the wife of a prince who had a mortal feud" against Hygelac for killing his father Ongentheow, ie Onela? Not necessarily, Tolkien replied, for at exactly this time Hygelac was very much in his prime, while the Swedish king was not yet Onela but Ohthere—whose death would cause the rebellion of his sons against Onela, something which takes place only in the post-Hygelac reign of Heardred. Putting all that together, as the poet does not bother to do, then at the moment of Beowulf's arrival at Heorot, Onela is very small beer, "a prince of a diminished house, merely the brother of a small king who had in any case two sons."

In fact, Tolkien argued, one might say that the poet's really brilliant stroke was inserting his fairy-tale hero into Scandinavian politics *at exactly the right time.*[14] One might crudely say, just before the roof fell in for the Danes and the Geats and, for a while, the Swedes as well. All of which provided a suitable political background for the poet's main theme, the contrast played out in Beowulf's own life between confident and optimistic youth and resigned, defiant old age

Of course, and once again (see pp. 22, 38, and 50 above), these overlapping hints of real-world politics could just be another coincidence! Or like the profusion of unnecessary names and the wealth of untold stories, they could all be "literary art" of the highest order, stuffed in like the clues in a modern detective story, whose significance you are only supposed to note once the solution has been given in the last chapter.

Leaving aside such issues, however, what all this suggests in terms of historical narrative is that the sequence of events

---

14 Tolkien, *Beowulf: A Translation and Commentary*, 219–20, 157.

above came rather close together, with continuous oscillations in the Scandinavian balance of power. It would be rash to put dates on any of this (though Tolkien did not hesitate to do so, see page 117 below). Still, if one rejects the fifty-year reign of (mythical) King Beowulf, such evidence as we have indicates that the "long vendetta" of Swedes and Geats took place earlier in the century rather than later: while the decisive period for the future of the Geats must have been the second quarter of the century, approx. 525–550.

The Migration-Period Crisis in Scandinavia

One has to ask again whether there is any archaeological corroboration for this whole story of the Geat–Swede vendetta, since there is so little in the way of outside documentation. The question is tied up with what some have called "the migration-period crisis." The term was discussed at length in a 1985 symposium on "The Migration Period in the North: a time of crisis between earlier and later Iron Ages."[15] This argued that there was a long depression over much of Scandinavia, starting close to the year 540 (the traditional boundary between earlier and later Germanic Iron Ages), and signalled by abandonment of settlements and a fall in population, as well as the dearth of rich graves already noted, p. 28 above.

The theory is not universally accepted, some sceptics sayng that every period has its crisis, others arguing that some areas of Scandinavia were untroubled and that abandonment of farms may just mean that the population became more concentrated on the better land. Archaeology can tell us what, and even how, but is not so good at why. Nevertheless there are some straws in the wind, and a very big wind it was: indeed some would call it a perfect storm.

---

15 *Folkevandringstiden i Norden: En krisetid mellem ældre og yngre jernalder* [The Migration Period in the North: a time of crisis between the Early and Late Iron Ages], ed. Ulf Näsman and Jørgen Lund (Aarhus: Aarhus Universitetsforlag, 1988).

One major cause of crisis at exactly the time indicated is now all but certain. Evidence from ice cores, pollen counts, tree rings, all show that in the year 535, and again 539/40, and possibly yet again in 547, the world was hit by major volcanic eruptions. Professor Price thinks that the second of these was at Lake Ilopango in Central America, and notes that it is estimated to have thrown nearly ninety cubic kilometres of dust and ash into the atmosphere[16]—bigger than the Mount Tambora eruption which caused the "year without a summer" in 1815, bigger even than Krakatoa in 1883, and dwarfing the recent eruptions of Mount Saint Helens in 1980 and 2008. Even the relatively tiny eruption in Iceland in 2008 threw so much ash into the atmosphere as to disrupt air travel for weeks, and the Ilopango eruption was far, far bigger than that.

Exactly what happened can no longer be determined. Some think that the Ilopango eruption actually took place a century before, in 431,[17] and the site(s) of the other eruption(s) are not known (Iceland is a likely suspect, as is Krakatoa many centuries before 1883).[18] What is certain is the effect of the eruption(s): a dust-veil which blocked out the sun not for weeks but for years. Their effects were noted all over the world, by for instance the Byzantine historian Procopius, referring to the 536 dust-veil created by the 535 eruption, and even in Britain, where the same dust-veil is mentioned in one of the very few documents surviving from the sixth century there, the monk Gildas's *De excidio Britanniae*, "On the Downfall of Britain."[19] But the effects on high-latitude Scan-

---

16 Price, *The Children of Ash and Elm*, 75.

17 See Victoria C. Smith et al., "The magnitude and impact of the 431 CE Tierra Blanca Joven eruption of Ilopango, El Salvador," available at www.pnas.org/content/117/42/26061.

18 For the Krakatoa theory, see David Keys, *Catastrophe: An Investigation into the Origins of the Modern World* (London: Century, 1999), 274–78. Keys notes also (254) that tree-rings show that northwest Sweden had the second coldest summer for 1500 years in 536.

19 See Procopius, *History of the Wars* (bk. 4, chap. 14; ed. Dewing,

dinavia, with its short growing season and often marginal agriculture, were especially bad. It's thought that as much as fifty percent of the Scandinavian population died of hunger.[20] The years 536–540 must have felt to the starving like the *fimbulwinter*, the winter which never ends, and which in later Norse mythology presages Ragnarok, the end of the world.[21] (Ragnarok is normally understood as *ragna-rök*, "the doom of the gods," but Snorri, author of the main account of Old Norse myth, understood it as *ragna-rökkr*, "the twilight of the gods," and perhaps he was right.) And on top of it Scandinavia may have been reached by bubonic plague, which hit Byzantium in 541, and is known to have spread as far as north Germany: as with the much later Black Death, trade contacts spread the plague very efficiently.

There is no mention of either disease or famine in *Beowulf*, which sees the whole history of the years before and after the Hygelac disaster (approx. 520 on) in terms of dynastic struggle, and remembers above all dramatic incidents of battle and revenge. The *Beowulf*-view is not incompatible with the scientific one, however. In his final summary on the "migration-period crisis" Professor Näsman admits many possible causes for what he sees as a major social collapse—climate change, soil exhaustion, over-population, social change, lost connections with Europe (etc.)—but amongst them he lists also *inre maktkamp*, "domestic power-struggles":[22] which is what *Beowulf* keeps telling us about.

2:329); chap. 93 of Gildas, *The Ruin of Britain and other Documents*, ed. and trans. Michael Winterbottom (London: Philimore, 1978), 90, and further Andrew Breeze, *British Battles 493-937: Mount Badon to Brunanburh* (London: Anthem, 2020), 5–7. Confirmation from other sources in Italy, Europe, and Asia is cited by Keys, *Catastrophe*, 251 ff.

20 Price, *The Children of Ash and Elm*, 76–82 (50 percent estimate at 77).

21 A connection made by Bo Gräslund, "Fimbulvintern, Ragnarök och klimatkrisen år 536–537 e. Kr" [The Fimbulwinter, Ragnarok and the Climate Crisis of 536-7 CE], *Saga och Sed* (2007): 93–123.

22 Ulf Näsman, "Den folkvandringstida ?krisen i Sydskandinavien,

Professor Näsman is also careful, as historians and archae-ologists are, to say that different conclusions can be drawn from different locations, and that more complex models will be required for full understanding—in the academic world, you never lose points for saying "more research is needed." So it's fair to ask whether we have any more targeted studies on the Geatish/Swedish border? And as it happens we do.

This is Martin Rundkvist's thorough and painstaking study of *The Mead-Halls of the Eastern Geats*—a rather paradoxical title, since as we're told by Professor Rundkvist (University of Lódz, Poland), when his book was written, we didn't know of any. "Not one of the Beowulfian mead-halls of this book's title—being my shorthand for the ostentatious manorial buildings where the Late Iron Age elite lived their lives and played their roles—has been identified in the field...we do not have the floor-plan of a single mead-hall in the province [of East Gotland]."[23] And these days (as Professor Herschend has made very clear, see p. 20 above), you can't say you've found an elite settlement unless you can point to its hall.

Halls, however, survive only as post-holes in the ground, not readily visible. Thirty years ago no-one knew that even the giant Lejre halls were there, while the post-holes of the Anglo-Saxon royal palace at Yeavering in Northumbria were discovered only by aerial photography in an unusually dry year, and this in spite of the fact that the site was actually named in Bede's *History* of 731! So what Professor Rund-kvist's book did was to search out signs of elite settlement by plotting all archaeological finds made in the area and from the right period, and then note clusters for further investi-gation. (It is a pleasure to report that the search has been successful, uncovering a "real-world correlate of the *Beowulf* poem's royal mead-hall Heorot.")[24]

---

inklusive Öland och Gotland," in *Folkevandringstiden i Norden*, ed. Näsman and Lund, 227–55 at 250.

23 Rundkvist, *Mead-Halls of the Eastern Geats*, 9.

24 Rundkvist, *Mead-Halls of the Eastern Geats*, 35–37 for "clusters,"

Professor Rundkvist moreover is in no doubt that the land of the Eastern Geats underwent in the period under discussion something like a "demographic and economic collapse...the mid-6th century must have been a highly stressful time." What is especially interesting are the signs at this time of discontinuity. There is reasonable continuity, Rundkvist reports, from the Late Roman Period (150–400) through to the Migration Period (375–540), but much less (only in four parishes out of twenty-two) from the Migration Period through to the Vendel Period (540–790). What happened in the early-to-mid sixth century? We have no idea, but East Gothland is on the edge of the Beowulfian combat zone with the Swedes, bordered by the great Lake Vätter, with to the west Lake Väner, where they fought the battle on the ice. Rundkvist says rather grimly, "Vendel Period elite families most likely did not inherit power from their Migration Period forebears in an undramatic fashion."[25]

That's not what happens in Heroic Ages. The hall at Uppåkra near Lund, in Skåne to the south of East and West Gotland, was burned down three times between 400 and 600, at least once with people still inside: marks on their bones show that the bodies were left in the ruins for dogs to gnaw.[26] At the end of *Beowulf* the Messenger who announces the hero's death also looks forward to a future where there will be no-one to bury the dead, left for wolf, eagle, and raven. (But being eaten on the battlefield by "the beasts of battle"

---

and for the updated discovery, see Martin Rundkvist and Andreas Viberg, "Geophysical Investigations on the Viking-Period Mound at Aska in Hagebyhöga Parish, Sweden," *Archaeological Prospection* 22, no. 2 (2014): 131–38. The comparison with Heorot is in the initial "Abstract" (https://onlinelibrary.wiley.com/doi/abs/10.1002/arp.1500).

25 Rundkvist, *Mead-Halls of the Eastern Geats*, 39 ("stressful"), 46 ("undramatic").

26 Lars Larsson, "Mordutredning pågår i Uppåkra" [Murder-Investigation Ongoing in Uppåkra"], *Populär Arkeologi* 27, no. 1 (2009): 14–15 at 15.

could at least be considered a heroic ending: being left in the ashes of your own home for stray dogs is just sad and squalid.) Professor Herschend, quoted several times already, sums up the sixth-century situation: "in the middle of the [first] millennium" the region went "down to hell."[27]

Three Contradictions

The poet's focus is firmly on the three royal dynasties of eastern Scandinavia, Danes, Swedes, and Geats, who—like the famous Kilkenny cats—fought each other until only the tails were left. He is nevertheless aware, even unexpectedly aware, of what in the mid-sixth century was Scandinavia's "open frontier" to the west: the Jutes, the Frisians, the Franks.

But where were the Angles and the Saxons? One of the strangest things about *Beowulf* is the way that the poem itself contradicts all the things that we think we know about the poet. Almost universal opinion now—no opinion about *Beowulf* is ever universal—is that the poet was literate (his poem is a written epic, not the record of an oral composition); he was also a Christian (which goes very much with being literate, in post-Roman northwest Europe); and that he was English (because the poem is written in Old English).

If you look at the poem itself, however, though God is mentioned many times and reference is also made to the Bible stories of Cain and Abel and (more indirectly) Noah's flood, the name of Christ never appears, nor are words such as "Saviour" or "Redeemer" ever used. Of course the poem is set in a pre-Christian milieu, but this did not stop other Anglo-Saxon poets, like the author of *Judith*, next poem in the manuscript to *Beowulf*, and set in Old Testament times, from using Christian language freely.

---

27 Herschend, quoted in Giorgio Ausenda, "Current Issues and Future Directions in the Study of the Scandinavians: Summary of participants' discussions and comments," in *The Scandinavians from the Vendel Period to the Tenth Century: An Ethnographic Perspective*, ed. Judith Jesch (Woodbridge: Boydell, 2002), 321–53 at 333.

As for literacy, the poet seems to know very little about it. He uses the verb *writan* twice in the poem, but it means "cut, engrave," which is what it meant when all writing was in runic script cut or carved on to wood or stone. When Beowulf kills the dragon, he *forwrat* or "forwrote" it, that is, he "cut it through" or "cut it down." When he gives Hrothgar the sword-hilt retrieved from the underwater cave (the blade has melted), on it is *writen* the story of how the Flood drowned the race of giants. It seems unlikely that a whole text could be "written" on a sword-hilt. More likely what's meant is an engraved picture, while the *runstafas* or runic letters also mentioned just give, perhaps, the name of the smith who forged it (a common use for runes).

The most annoying discrepancy, however, to nineteenth-century scholars intent on discovering a truly national epic, was that the poet seemed never to have heard of England, or Britain, and to have no interest in either. Nor was he as interested as he should be in his own tribal ancestry. There are only five names in the poem belonging to anyone who could be regarded, at a stretch, as English ancestors, and all fall into the category of "exceptions that prove a rule": the rule being, total ignorance of and lack of interest in English national origins.

One of the names is Offa, the name of the famous King of Mercia in the seventh century, builder of "Offa's Dyke." The name was presumably chosen (or adopted) to give him legitimacy and gain the reflected glory of the man he claimed as an ancestor, a much earlier Offa. It is this earlier Offa who is mentioned in the poem, and in a way which has given scholars a lot of anxiety.

What the poem says, at some length (lines 1926b–62), is that Hygelac's wife, Hygd, was everything a queen ought to be. Not at all like another queen, who was in the habit of having men executed for looking at her! But even the wicked queen was reformed. "The ale-drinkers," no doubt gossiping in the mead-hall, "told another tale" about her, once she was given in marriage to Offa, who "put a stop to" her bad habits, so that she too became a model wife and mother. It sounds awfully like a "taming of the shrew" story, which makes modern scholars nervous, and they are especially nervous about the term translated here as "put a stop to," *onhohsnode*, which looks very like a word for "hamstrung," the *hohsinu* being the "hough-sinews" or hamstrings. (One hopes that this was not meant literally.) Offa, nevertheless, whatever he did, gets nine lines of praise, along with mention of three of his relatives, including Eomer—a name prominent in Mercian royal ancestry (which is why Tolkien, a loyal Mercian, picked it up for one of his major fictional characters), but which scribe B failed to understand, writing in its place the there-meaning-less adjective *geomor*, "sad."

This early Offa, Offa I, has his own story, which makes one of the little vignettes in *Widsith*. He fixed the southern boundary of the Angles by fighting a duel on an island in the river Eider against two champions of the *Swæfe*, the Swabians, and he fought one-against-two to wipe out the shame of two Angles fighting a single Swabian (thus establishing the tradition of *le fair-play anglais*). But the Eider is in Jutland, not England. At the time of Offa I the Angles had not yet emigrated to Britain. They were still in their home on the European continent, so the "no mention of England" rule still applies, to Offa and his three named relatives.

As for the Saxons, they never appear in the poem at all. However, all is not quite lost, for Bede notoriously claimed that England, as we now know it, was settled by the Angles, Saxons, and Jutes. These would better be remembered as, north to south, the Jutes, Angles, and Saxons, with (now going south to north) (1) the Saxons down by the river Elbe; (2) the Angles in "the Angle" or *Angeln*, the corner of land between the river Schlei and Flensborg Fjord, now just south of the modern Danish/German border (as remembered by Tolkien, who had his three tribes of hobbits immigrate into the Shire from a similar if fictional Angle between the rivers Hoarwell and Loudwater); and (3) the Jutes to the north of them above the modern border.

Beowulf does show a strong interest in the Jutes, and their temporary leader Hengest—at last, a name familiar, along with his brother Horsa, from English legend and even English history, both of them even commemorated on the Great Seal of the United States of America! Any premature relief, however, is checked immediately by the fact that there is no mention of Horsa in the poem—both Hengest and Horsa are words for "horse"—and that what we are told about the Jutes there is even more puzzling than the rest of the poem. (It does not help that the tribal name *Eotan*, "the Jutes," is very like the common noun *eoten*, *eotenas*, "giant, giants," fantasy-fans very much preferring to choose the latter option whenever they can.) But in spite of everything, what we are told in the poem about the Jutes does fit very well with what Professor Anderson cautiously called, see p. 3 above, "the pattern of Scandinavian history."

The Problem of the Jutes

The Jutes, obviously, come from Jutland, most of which is now part of Denmark. The rest of modern Denmark consists of the Danish archipelago to the east of Jutland, especially the two big islands, west to east, of Funen and Sjælland. Lejre, where Heorot may have been, is on the northeast corner of Sjælland, not far from Copenhagen, almost as far from Jutland as you can get and still be in Denmark.

In brief, the Danes, or people who would eventually come to be called the Danes, seem to have moved, far back near the start of the Christian era, out of what is now Skåne in southern Sweden, into Sjælland, perhaps evicting the Heruls or *Eorle*, and maybe the *Beardan* or Bards as well, rolling up the smaller tribes by taking away their mead-settles and smashing their mead-halls, crossing the Great Belt to take over the island of Funen—and eventually finding themselves confronting the Jutes of Jutland across the water of what is now called the Little Belt.

We now know that it was the destiny of the Jutes to become part of Denmark. But it seems, in *Beowulf*, that no-one has yet persuaded them of this. Or not all of them, anyway.

The first time the Jutes appear in the poem is in connection with the deposition of Heremod, suggested at the start of this book to be the cause of the interregnum which brings Scyld and the Scyldings into Danish history. In lines 901-15 Beowulf, having defeated Grendel, is compared favourably with Heremod. He too, we are told, had been expected to be a "cure for afflictions," and the Danes had high hopes of him. But in some unspecified way Heremod went to the bad, and was (lines 902b–904a) "misled, sent away, into the power of enemies, among the Jutes"—or "among the giants"? More details are given later on by Hrothgar, who says that he was a great champion, but bloodthirsty: he killed his own companions, he was stingy with rings as well, and in the end (lines 1714b–1715a) he "turned alone from the joys of men." Very much reading between the lines, perhaps he was deposed for his tyranny and his meanness, and fled into exile among the Jutes.

The Jutes figure also, but not much clearer as things stand, in the song which is sung in Hrothgar's hall after the defeat of Grendel, and of which we are given a summary, usually described as "the Finnsburg Episode." Unusually, in fact uniquely, we have another Old English poem which describes the same event, and has been given the title "The Fight at Finnsburg." Interpreting these two, and relating them to each other, has probably caused more dispute than anything else in Old English studies—very largely, one might well think, from motives of national pride.

One reason why *Beowulf* was such a disappointment to English scholars like W. P. Ker and R. W. Chambers (whom Tolkien picked out for criticism in his 1936 lecture) was that it did not offer the kind of human drama found in other Germanic legends, like the Nibelung story or the story of Walter (Waldhere) from Aquitaine, drama which centred on strife between kin, divided loyalties, oathbreaking: indeed, as Professor Leonard Neidorf points out,[28] at the end of his life Beowulf congratulates himself specifically on never having been guilty of any of that! The Finnsburg story, however,

---

28 Neidorf, Leonard, "The *Beowulf*-Poet's Sense of Decorum," *Traditio* 76 (2021): 1–28.

involved all these themes. And what made it in its turn unpalatable was that it was clear that in it *someone* had behaved badly, even dishonourably. Worse still, for English scholars, one of them might have been, if not an Englishman (since these did not yet exist), at least an English ancestor and a figure in the national myth of origins: Hengest, first invader of England, and legendary founder of the kingdom of Kent. Surely such a person could not be charged with "ungentlemanly conduct"?

The situation at the start of the Finnsburg story is fairly clear. A group of "Half-Danes" (*Healf-dene*) are visiting the court of Finn, son of Folcwalda, king of the Frisians, who live to the south of Jutland on the North Sea coast, their territory possibly extending further to the north towards Jutland than it does at present. The leader of the Half-Danes is Hnæf son of Hoc, and he is the brother of Hildeburh, married to Finn, and mother of a child who is already of fighting age—all of which suggests that the Half-Danes, whoever they are, have been concerned to make alliance with the Frisians.

But the Half-Danes are attacked, at night and treacherously, in the hall which has been assigned to them as living-quarters. The "Fragment" poem begins with a watchman calling attention to something (is it fire?), and being answered, in Tolkien's opinion by Hnæf himself, who tells him, what he's seen isn't dawn, it isn't a dragon flying, it isn't fire—what it is, is "woeful deeds arising." What the watchman has seen is the glint of moonlight on drawn weapons, and Hnæf immediately calls his men to stand to.

None of this is in the summary in *Beowulf* (lines 1066a–1159, in which line 1069 further identifies Hnæf as a Scylding). This begins not with details of the night-attack, but with the despair of Hildeburh the following morning, when she wakes to find "killing of kinsmen" on both sides—her brother Hnæf on one side, her unnamed son (probably) on the other[29]—and

---

29 One would expect a son to side with his father Finn, but the tie between mother's brother and sister's son was especially strong in Anglo-Saxon culture, so maybe the unnamed son sided with his

what seems now to be an uneasy stand-off. The "Episode" in fact is concerned with what happens after the attack, and once again the purely tactical situation seems clear. The Half-Danes have held out in the hall, and Finn has had heavy casualties. He cannot finish them off, but conversely they cannot break out. (This seems obvious, because if either side *could* finish the others off, they would.) Moreover Hnæf has been killed in the fighting, as has the son of Finn and Hildeburh, and there is a long description of their cremation. The Half-Danes' leader is now Hengest.

So the deal is now that there will be a truce between Finn and Hengest and their respective followers. The Half-Danes will have their own accommodation over the winter—for the weather prevents them from sailing home—and will get equal treatment from Finn. A particular provision of the treaty is that *no-one* is to reproach any of the Half-Danes for now taking service with the *bana* of their lord, the man responsible for his death, that is to say, with Finn. They have (presumably in some views) done something dishonourable in not fighting on till they were all dead but instead taking a new oath of loyalty. So if any of the Frisians (*Frysna*) says anything about it, that will be a capital offence.

And there is the crux for modern English scholars. Hengest has a prominent role in both "Episode" and "Fragment"—in the latter, when Hnæf orders the stand-to, five warriors are named as they go to guard the doors, but Hengest is the one who gets a line to himself. If he *was* the same man as England's legendary founder, and the man who makes the deal with Finn: well, this does not look good. ("Perfidious Albion" from the very start, some might say.)

But what about the night-attack? Surely that was also perfidious? But who made it? Right at the start of the "Episode" it says that Hildeburh "had no need to praise the good faith of the Jutes (*Eotena*)." In other words, this was all the fault

uncle Hnæf? Uncle and nephew are cremated side by side, lines 1114–17.

of the bad faith of the Jutes, not the Frisians. Later on the Half-Danes are promised equal treatment with both Jutes and Frisians, so the two latter groups are quite distinct. And when the truce is finally broken, by Hengest—who is now guilty of oath-breaking as well as surrender-on-terms—the Jutes are mentioned twice as Hengest's real target, though Finn is killed as well. Hildeburh is furthermore rescued, if rescue it is, and taken back to Denmark. As sung in Hrothgar's hall, the "Episode" is a song of Danish triumph.

Except that Hengest and the others in the hall are only Half-Danes. And the relationship between Jutes and Frisians is unknown. As is what started the trouble and triggered the night-attack in the first place. And above all, there is the fact that if Hengest is the same man as the legendary founder of Kent—and there are only two people in all our records with the same name, and the dates fit—the Hengest who was the founder of Kent is early identified as *being a Jute himself.*

This has proved over the decades, to use the modern phrase, to be a real can of worms. R. W. Chambers, with whom Tolkien disagreed on this issue, but whom he also regarded as his friend and to some extent his mentor, spent many pages working out an acceptable answer, in which at the end no individual could be blamed, and especially not Hengest-who-could-almost-be-considered-English: in Chambers's scenario, the killing of Hnæf was the fault of nameless and motiveless Jutes, so Hengest doing a deal with Finn the Frisian was reasonable, while the killing of Finn was in turn done by Danish reinforcements, nothing (well, not much) to do with Hengest, and national pride was saved...[30] At the cost of leaving several questions unanswered, besides the ones mentioned here.[31]

---

30 Chambers, *Beowulf: An Introduction to the Study of the Poem*, 283–87.

31 One being, what snaps Hengest's self-control at the end of the "bloodstained winter" during which he is obliged by weather to remain at Finnsburg, keeping the peace with Finn. In one interpretation of lines 1143–45, the *hildeleoma*, or "battle-light" with

Tolkien's Solution to the Problem of the Jutes

To all this embarrassing confusion, Tolkien offered a strikingly ingenious and attractive solution, which makes the point once again that he really—when not sticking up for fantasy—took *Beowulf* as a historical document very seriously indeed. This was published, nine years after his death, edited from his notes by Professor Alan Bliss, as *Finn and Hengest*. Regrettably, the book has made almost no mark on *Beowulf*-scholarship, first because Tolkien's 1936 denunciation of history had already made such a deep impression, but also because working out Tolkien's real meaning, in *Finn and Hengest*, from his clutter of notes on texts and names, is by no means easy: his problem, as he confessed, was that he was always a "niggler," a stickler for detail, and sometimes as time went by, for Tolkien, the details drowned the thought.

Putting it briefly, however, and considering the story historically, Tolkien's argument is that while Hnæf himself was a Dane and a Scylding, most or all of his men, Hengest included, were Jutes. The Danes had already started their take-over of the Jutes and Jutland, and the "Half-Danes" are either mixed-ethnicity, or, possibly, if the name was used contemptuously, Jutes who have given in to the Danes. In familiar World War 2 terms, some considered the likes of Hengest as "quislings," collaborators with a foreign invader, as represented by Hnæf himself.

Meanwhile, at Finn's court, and continuing to use anachronistic World War 2 terms, there is a group of what we might call "Free Jutes in Exile," who still have hopes of regaining their country. Naturally the two politically-opposed groups of Jutes hate each other even more than they hate anyone else. That is what motivates first the night-attack, and then the breach of the carefully-worked out peace-treaty.

---

which he is presented is the name of Hnæf's sword, shown to him as a silent reminder of his duty to take vengeance: another case of dead men's swords causing trouble when recognized, see also p. 41.

Tolkien also thought that a character who momentarily takes the stage in the "Fragment" was of special importance, one Garulf. He is among the attackers, and one of the other attackers is trying to hold him back, not risk his life (not a usual situation in the heroic world). Of course he takes no notice and instead calls out to know who is defending the hall-door against him: it is Sigeferth of the Secge, who gives his name and answers with something like the traditional war-cry of the modern English football hooligan, "Come on if you think you're hard enough." To which there is only one answer in the heroic world. Garulf attacks the door, and is killed, first to fall. (It's not inconsistent that Garulf is also identified as "son of Guthlaf," and Guthlaf is one of the hall's defenders. Perhaps Garulf wanted an assurance that he was not facing his own father.)

Tolkien's theory, however, was that Garulf was son not of Guthlaf but of Guthwulf, or possibly Gefwulf—we know the "Fragment" only from a poor eighteenth-century copy, since lost, so it is riddled with errors—which would make him, according once more to *Widsith, the rightful king of the Jutes*. That was why his men were trying to keep him out of harm's way, because with his death fell the last hopes of Jutish independence. It was a "Last of the Mohicans" situation.[32]

Tolkien's solution deserves to be better-known, and it has actually been put with great clarity in a Young Adult novel, *Hengist's Tale*, written by the novelist Jill Paton Walsh—who happens to be the niece of Alan Bliss, Tolkien's editor, and has kindly informed me that while up at Oxford she was in fact tutored by Tolkien. So there are two ways in which she could have learned of Tolkien's theory, and decided to fictionalize it, which I'm sure would have pleased Tolkien very much.

Its attraction here, meanwhile, is that once again, it fits the "pattern of Scandinavian history." The story belongs to a time when the Danes had taken over the Danish archipelago, and made a start on taking over Jutland, perhaps by diplomatic marriage into the royal family of the Hocings—Hnæf

---

32 Tolkien, *Finn and Hengest*, 33 (under heading "Garulf"), 159–60.

is identified as both a Hocing and a Scylding. This takeover, however, is still meeting resistance, possibly stamped out for good by "the fight at Finnsburg." As for what that time was, all we can say is that according to *Beowulf*, it is an event well in the past at the time of Beowulf's arrival at Hrothgar's hall, when Hygelac is still alive and in his prime. It belongs to the fifth century rather than the sixth, which is not inconsistent with the later career of Hengest, if he had one: see further p. 104ff. below.

Whatever its date, the fight must certainly have been an important event in history or in legend, for not only do we have two Old English poems about it, but—very oddly—it was also remembered for many years far away in Bavaria. There, as proved by Dr. Carl Hammer, a noble family, generation after generation, called its sons after the Finnsburg heroes, Hoc and Hnæf.[33] Bavaria is a very long way away from Frisia, but Dr. Hammer suggests that the story was brought there by Anglo-Saxon missionaries. It must have made a strong impression, for reasons we do not know.

One final coda is that Tolkien thought he personally might have had family connections with the story as well: he believed that the surname of his Aunt Jane Neave (who lived at a farm called "Bag End") could have been derived from *Hnæf*. The stories and the heroes live on, even if people don't notice them.

The Franks and the Frisians

The Frisians are also mentioned repeatedly in the poem's five accounts of or allusions to the Hygelac disaster. Both *Beowulf* and the anonymous Frankish chronicle (see p. 9 above) agree that this attack was made on the *Hetware* or *Attoarii*, who lived between the Maas and the Rhine in a district later called (in Dutch) the *Hettergouw*. On the other hand, in four of the

---

33 Carl I. Hammer, "Hnæf and Hoc in Bavaria: Early Medieval Prosopography and Heroic Poetry," *Medieval Prosopography* 26 (2005): 13–50.

five poetic mentions in *Beowulf*, the raid is said to have been directed at the Frisians, while the Franks are also mentioned twice, as are the *Hugas*, though this is thought to be an old name for the Franks.

Some of this is explicable. The *Attoarii* were clearly a people on the fringes of the Frankish Empire, incapable of resisting the Geatish raid themselves, but able to call on help from the Frankish king—who, as mentioned before, sent his son to the rescue very promptly. Modern Friesland, on the other hand, is some distance from the *Hettergouw*, and the Frisians were *not* part of the Frankish Empire, but remained determinedly independent for centuries. In the poem, the Messenger who announces Beowulf's death to the Geats says there will be trouble as soon as their king's death becomes known "to the Franks and Frisians" (*Froncum ond Frysum*), but it is not clear why the Frisians should be involved. Very likely the Frisians were the people of the North Sea seaboard best-known to Anglo-Saxons, and were brought into the story accordingly.

The poet, however, is curiously well-informed about the Franks, in one point at least better-informed than any ancient authority we know of, and *better-informed than modern historians*. It is a very strange fact that of all the hundreds of ancient texts which mention the dynasty which ruled the Franks from approxiamtely 450 to 751, *Beowulf* is *the only one which gets the name of its founder correct* (though "translated" from Old Frankish into Old English).

This is so odd that it needs some explanation. The name of the almost-mythical founder, corresponding to Danish Scyld, was *Merowech* (the asterisk indicates once again that this form is a supposition, or reconstruction, never exactly recorded). Why think that was his name? Because Gregory of Tours, in his *History of the Franks* already mentioned several times, gives it as *Merovechus*.[34] Gregory ought to have known, because he knew personally the man's grandson, who had been given the same name as his grandfather. Discounting

---

34 Gregory of Tours, *The History of the Franks*, trans. Thorpe, bk. 2, end of chap. 9, 125.

the -us ending, which writers in Latin tag on to barbarians' names (Chlochilaicus, Hiorvarthus etc.), we are left with what looks like a regular two-part Germanic name, *Mero-vech*. *Vech*, however, doesn't mean anything plausible in a Germanic language: the Wikipedia entry on the name suggests it's a mistake for *vecht* or "fight," but that's just hopeful.

It's already been mentioned that writers in Latin had no letter for "w," and had different ways of getting round this, one of them being to substitute "v" (see p. 9 above). **Mero-wech* fits much better as a likely name. The first element means "sea" (and Gregory has a strange tale about Merowech's mother being impregnated by a sea-monster), and the second, in its Old English form *weoh* or *wioh*, means "holy place, pagan temple," or more narrowly, "pagan idol"— it survives in modern German *weihen*, "to consecrate," and more familiarly in *Weihnacht*, "Holy Night" or Christmas Eve. It is also related to the first element in Latin *victima* (in Classical Latin pronounced "wiktima"), which originally meant "animal for sacrifice." Early kings were priest-kings as well, and one of their roles was sacrificing for the people.

In newly-converted Anglo-Saxon England, however, the word's pagan meanings made it unpopular, and it fell out of use—except in place-names like Weedon or Weoley, and personal names, see below—or else it was confused with the common word *wig*, "war." Near the start of *Beowulf* the poet says that the pagan Danes, in their despair over Grendel, resorted to idol-worship, and scribe A has written it as *wigweorþung*, but it's obvious from context that the poet meant *wioh*-. The word also survived as a name-element, as in Weohstan, the most famous example however being King Oswy, or Oswig, or Oswiu, who ruled in favour of the Roman Church as opposed to the Irish Church at the Synod of Whitby in 664. Good Christian though the king was, and variably as his name is spelled, his name was really **Oswioh*, and it originally meant "pagan god" (*Os-*) + "pagan shrine / idol" (*-wioh*): names are kept when their meanings have been lost.

The first Frankish king, then, was Mero-wech, probably "sea-shrine," and if one adds the regular -ing ending to show "descent from," then his dynasty ought to be called the "Meroweching" dynasty. But it wasn't, and isn't. As said above, p. 9, writers in Latin had trouble with the sounds "w" and "ch," having no letters for either, and the habit became established of writing either *Merovingi* (which gets the -w wrong and misses out the -ch) or *Merohingi* (which has trouble with the -ch and misses out the -w). As the dynasty faded from memory, guesses at the name got even worse, *Meronigi, Merohinchi, Morahinguorum, Merungum*...Modern historians have fixed on "Merovingian" as standard, and I keep it here for the sake of familiarity. But all the ancient uses, and all the modern ones as well, are *wrong.*

Which makes it so surprising that the *Beowulf*-poet, uniquely, got it *right.* Though it's significant that scribe B (writing 250 years after the last Merovingian king was deposed) had no idea what he meant.

The vital reference appears in line 2921. This is near the start of the long speech, the longest in the poem (lines 2900–3027), in which the Messenger announces Beowulf's death, looks back over recent history, and makes a gloomy prophecy about the future. The speech is beautifully shaped—one can see why everyone is so sure this has to be a written epic. After announcing the death, the Messenger says there will be trouble once this is known to the "Franks and Frisians"; nor can one expect anything but trouble from the Swedes, as a result of the old hostility going back to the killings of Hæthcyn and Ongentheow, which he details with great vigour; he sums up by saying that hostility is what the Geats must now expect. They will get only "feud and enmity" from the Swedes. As for the Franks, ever since the Hygelac raid, says the Messenger, "the favour of the Merovingian" has not been given to us.

Scribe B could not understand this at all (both he and scribe A had continual problems with names). He made nonsense of it, but—bless his long-dead heart—what he did was scrupulously copy the letters he saw before him, making only one mistake, but totally ruining the word-division. The manuscript reads, quite clearly, *mere wio ingasmilts,* the last "word" in particular making no sense. What the poet meant was (no capital letters for names in Old English) *merewioinges milts*, *milts* meaning "mildness" or "kindness" or "favour." The form of the name however shows that the poet has (a) "translated" Frankish *Mero-* to Old English *Mere-* (b) "translated" Frankish *-wech* to Old English *-wioh*, both correctly, and also, and again correctly, (c) remembered that in Old English a final -h is dropped before a following -ing—so that, for instance, King Oswioh's son is listed in Anglo-Saxon genealogies as Ecgfrith Osweoing.

As said above, everybody else got the name wrong, the *Beowulf*-poet got it right...This very surprising fact has a bearing on the vexed question of the date when the poem was written. Since the poet could not have got the name-form from any written text we know of, and since it would have been very difficult for him to work it out from the garbled forms in those written texts, then the simple explanation is that the poet knew the correct form of the name of the dynasty because it was still in use.

This would also explain why he equates "king of the Franks" with "Merovingian" without having to explain to his audience, for instance, that "while the king of the Franks isn't a Merovingian now (we all know they've been replaced by the Carolingians), they were back *then*, at the time I'm talking about." Instead, the poet and his original audience were quite happy to hear the king of the Franks called "the Merovingian" because, at the time of writing, he *was*, and as far as they knew, *he always had been*, since, literally, time immemorial. The correct name of the dynasty must surely have been current while it held the throne, not in writing but in speech. How long it remained current after the dynasty was deposed in 751 is guesswork: but probably not long. The Carolingians who succeeded had a vested interest, like all usurpers, in blotting out memory of their takeover.

Nevertheless, leaving the date issue aside, it's striking that the poet is well-informed about the name, and about the Frankish language. (One other text, the *Life of Saint Wilfrid* written in the North of England about 710, also "translates" all Frankish names automatically into their Old English equivalents, but this is unusual, and the *Life* is written in Latin.) And there is one other example of such "translation" in the poem, which is almost equally surprising.

This comes before the dragon-fight. Beowulf makes three speeches, sitting outside the dragon's lair. As mentioned already, they perhaps give the impression that he is "psyching himself up" for the fight to come, which he knows he is unlikely to survive. He looks back over his life, remembering his many battles, and congratulating himself for his long service to his uncle Hygelac. Hygelac had no need to call on foreign champions, says Beowulf, because he, Hygelac's nephew, was always there, "ever since I killed Dæghrefn, champion of the Hugas, bare-handed...the edge did not kill him, but my war-grip broke his house-of-bones (*banhus*), the pulses of his heart," lines 2501–8a. (The name Beowulf has long been interpreted as "Wolf of the Bees," i.e., the honey-loving bear, with Beowulf as a Bear's Son, and this has now been challenged.[35] This particular exploit nevertheless sounds very like a bearhug. What can *banhus* mean but "rib-cage," and if you crush that the snapped ribs will certainly pierce the heart?)

Be that as it may, the interesting name here is Dæghrefn, "Day-raven." Just like Heorogar (see p. 51 above), this is not an Anglo-Saxon name, but where Heorogar's name was early Scandinavian, Dæghrefn is a Frankish name, even a characteristically Frankish name. "Day" names are fairly common in Old English but also well-known in Frankish, as with the three Merovingian kings called Dagobert. "Raven" as a name-element, however, is practically unknown in Old English: the website PASE (Prosopography of Anglo-Saxon England) lists fifteen among its thousands of mentions of real-life Anglo-Saxon names, but all but one (*Wæl-hrafn*) belong to either Frankish or Norse immigrants. In Frankish, however, "Raven"

---

35 By R. D. Fulk, "The Etymology and Significance of Beowulf's Name," *Anglo-Saxon England* 1 (2007): 109–36. Fulk sees the name not as Beo-wulf ("wolf of the bees") but as Beow-(w)ulf, "follower of the god Beow."

is common as a first element, as a second element, or on its own: respectively *Chramnesindus* ("Raven-companion," the name of a malefactor in Gregory's *Historiae*), *Wulfhramn* ("Wolf-raven," the saintly missionary to the Frisians), and *Chramn* (just-plain "Raven," a prince in Gregory, as also the famous Frankish abbot Hrabanus Maurus).

Once again we have the usual two options. We can think that the poet made the name up, cunningly using elements he knew were at once Frankish, for local colour, and comprehensible, so his audience would get the point: cunningly also laying no stress on his invention, to create the "reality effect" (Tolkien's "literary art" here once more clearly exposed). Or we can, as before, take the simpler option. Everything to do with Beowulf is admittedly fiction (thirty suits of armour, fifty-year reign etc.), including this feat on a historical battlefield. But conceivably Dæghrefn *was* the name of a Frankish champion of the Heroic Age, well-enough known in legend for his name to be remembered—like Vesteinn / Weohstan, see p. 66 above—and the poet borrowed it. As it happens, "Dayraven" is recorded twice in Continental European documents, though in monastic not military contexts: *Dagaramnus*, *Daigramnus*.[36] (Of course, and for the fifth time, this could just be a coincidence.)

The poet, then, knew a lot about the Merovingian Franks. This makes what the Messnger says about them near the end of the poem, once Beowulf is dead, rather harder to interpret: lines 2920b–21, "[ever since the Hygelac raid] the favour of the Merovingian has not been given to us."

In context this sounds feeble. The Messenger is saying, "On our northern border the Swedes are preparing to come down on us, kill the men, enslave the women, and leave the bodies for the wolf and the eagle. And besides, five hundred miles away in Aachen, across the North Sea, with no known naval or military capacity to actually reach us, the king of the Franks is displeased."

---

36 See Shippey, "Names in *Beowulf* and Anglo-Saxon England," 66–67.

Surely he must mean something more than that. But to understand it one needs to understand the economic nature of "prestige societies": also known to some as "pillage societies," or "pirate societies."

Prestige Societies: Money, Mathoms, and Worth

There is no mention of money in *Beowulf*—with one doubtful and revealing exception. When Beowulf is announced to Hrothgar by his doorward, Wulfgar the Wendel, Hrothgar says that he has heard of this man already, from the Danes who some time ago—probably following the accession of Hygelac, see p. 71 above—took to the Geats *gifsceattas* from the Danes (line 378). In normal Old English, a *sceat* is a coin, defined (in Kent) as one twentieth part of a shilling, quite like a penny. But these are *gif-sceattas*, meant as gifts, and coins are unsuitable as gifts: too much like sending tribute-money, definitely not intended. These instead are what Hrothgar calls much later *luftacen* (line 1863), diplomatic "tokens of affection." It seems that money in *Beowulf* is like writing (see p. 77 above): the word is there, *writen* or *sceattas*, but it has not yet taken on its later and familiar meaning.

By contrast, repeatedly mentioned in *Beowulf*—about forty times, sometimes in compounds—are *maðmas*, the plural form of (variously spelled) *maððum*. These are constantly being donated. Hrothgar gives one to each of Beowulf's surviving companions after the Grendel fight, and gives Beowulf twelve more after his second fight, while Hygelac's wife Hygd is praised for the way she habitually gives them to the Geats. In fact, not only should they be given, they *must* be given. Hrothgar finishes his analysis of where people go wrong by saying that when a miser dies, his successor will "give out *madmas* lavishly," and (implied) quite right too. It's only monsters who hoard *maðmas*, particularly the dragon, a bad habit mentioned seven times, but also the Grendel-kin. After Beowulf defeated Grendel's mother in her underwater lair, he saw many *maðm-æhta*, "mathom-possessions," but he didn't take them: only Grendel's head and the hilt of the giant sword with which he beheaded both trolls, and he immediately donated both of these to Hrothgar.

But what are "mathoms"? The question occurred to Tolkien—most questions did—and he answered it jokingly at the start of *The Lord of the Rings*. It should be said that there is no money in *The Lord of the Rings* either, with again one interesting exception. The word is used fifteen times, but fourteen of those are linked with hobbits, or the Shire, or Barliman Butterbur, the innkeeper at Bree. (The fifteenth is in an Appendix.) But in the heroic world of Middle-Earth—as opposed to the Victorian England of the Shire, with its anachronistic tomatoes and potatoes, tobacco, and postal service—money does not figure. As for "mathoms," according to Tolkien, the Shire museum is called "the Mathom-house," and "anything that Hobbits had no immediate use for, but were unwilling to throw away, they called a *mathom*. Their dwellings were apt to become rather crowded with mathoms, and"—Tolkien informs us that hobbits loved giving and receiving presents—"many of the presents that passed from hand to hand were of that sort."[37]

Tolkien has got the main point about "mathoms," which is that they must circulate, but is joking about how they function in a society like the Shire's, which uses money. Shire-mathoms are like the bric-a-brac stall at a village fair. In *Beowulf*, *maðmas* are very different. But what are they? They may be made of gold. The massive golden neck-ring which Wealhtheow gives to Beowulf is definitely a *maððum*, just like the famous "necklace of the Brosings" made for the goddess Freyja by the dwarves. They are often old: Hrothgar sent *ealde maðmas* to the Wylfings as compensation for a killing done by Beowulf's father Ecgtheow. They may be imports: the *maðmas* piled up in Scyld's funeral boat come *of feorwegum*, "from far-off ways." Swords definitely count as *maðmas*, especially if old or family-possessions. When the old Heathobard warrior points out to the young one how a Dane is swanking with his father's sword, it's a *maððum*.

---

37 Tolkien, "Prologue" to *The Fellowship of the Ring*.

In brief, it looks as if *maðmas* can be more or less anything, as long as it is valuable, portable, and showy: rings, torques, necklaces, swords, cups, maybe (remembering the "smashed halls," see p. 21 above) Roman glassware. One way in which they may be passed on is not as gifts, but as loot: warriors carry their *maðmas* with them into battle, to be stripped from their dead bodies if they lose. That is what happens with Wealhtheow's golden torque.

Maðmas, however, unlike money, can't be spent. So what is the point of them? We get a very economical answer in a minor moment of the poem. Beowulf, on his way home from Denmark, meets once again the coastguard who challenged him on his arrival, showed him the way, and arranged for the care of his boat. He promptly gives him a sword, "bound with gold," so that the coastguard was ever after, line 1902, "because of the *maþm*, the worthier (*weorþra*) on the mead-bench."

It's obvious what this means. The sword gives the coastguard enhanced prestige, and the place where enhanced prestige is valuable is, of course, the meadbench in the mead-hall. (That's why meadbenches get taken away by conquerors, and mead-halls get smashed.)

It's also not hard to understand. We have *maðmas* as well—the expensive watch, the expensive car. Nevertheless the psychology has changed. For one thing, we have something of a taboo (stronger in some quarters than in others) against open flaunting of wealth: asking "how much are you worth?" would be regarded as rude. For another, we are more suspicious of display. In our culture, someone's financial worth may well be concealed, in a trust fund, in stocks and shares, in a property portfolio, while on the other hand all that gold jewellery may well be just bling. It's hard to recapture the anxiety which must have been there when your worth was on display all the time—and had to be kept topped up.

For *maðmas* worked two ways. After Beowulf is dead from dragon-bite, Wiglaf berates bitterly the thanes who did not come to his aid: the *maðmas* he gave them were wasted, and the penalties for that will be severe. Conversely, the lord who stops giving out *maðmas* will be deserted. He needs his thanes in order to gain more *maðmas*, by loot and piracy, or as *luftacen* from those who wish to show him respect; he needs the *maðmas* to increase his retinue of thanes; the thanes need ways to demonstrate their loyalty and earn more *maðmas*...And, on both sides, there's no way of hiding your resources or lack of them. The heroic world feels like a constant welter of challenge-and-response.

What may have made this constant anxiety over display and circulation of valuables especially strong in Scandinavia was that they had no home-grown source for them. Scandinavia had no resources in gold or silver, or garnets for their favourite jewellery. It all either had to come from the past—heirlooms or buried treasure, the one a diminishing resource, the other as unlikely then as now—or it had to come from the south: in fact, and to a large if unknown extent, in some periods, from Merovingian Gaul, where the kings had tight control on all such objects. And if the supply was cut off, then the whole "prestige economy" was at risk: nothing for the lords, nothing for the retainers.

And there are strong indications that that is what happened. The situation was not exactly what we would call trade. To quote Dr. Ljungkvist (yet again of Uppsala University), "The Scandinavian import of goods from the continent was completely geared to luxuries and objects that can be related to the expression of power"—in other words, *maðmas*. What was exported from Scandinavia is by contrast, "very hard to detect archaeologically."[38] Maybe the imported *maðmas* were just, so to speak, "sweeteners": a kind of informal protection money, a relatively cheap way of warding off raids like Hygelac's. But when that didn't work, well—that could be what the poet's Messenger meant by saying "the favour of the Merovingian has not been given to us." He cut

---

38 John Ljungkvist, "Continental Imports to Scandinavia," in *Foreigners in Early Medieval Europe: Thirteen Studies in Early Medieval Mobility*, ed. Dieter Quast (Mainz: Römisch-Germanisches Zentralmuseum, 2009), 27–49 at 27.

off the supplies. He created an economic crisis in the "prestige economy."

Is that what really happened? Once again, the archaeological record gives the poem strong support. In an exceptionally interesting paper Professor Martin Rundkvist—quoted already with regard to mead-halls—notes that in the post-Roman period, the fifth and early sixth centuries, "the ailing Roman Empire bled gold into northern Europe" (so the Dark Age for some was a Golden Age for others, see p. 28 above). The gold was not used as money, for there was at this time no money-economy: instead, "the gold gradually shed its monetary value and…acquired a strong supernatural glamour." Or, one might say, in the form of *maðmas*, became the great marker of prestige.

But then the Golden Age came to an end, as a result of the ascendancy of the Merovingian dynasty across the main routes of supply. By the middle of the sixth century—the era in which *Beowulf* is set—solid gold and silver become, in Sweden, "nearly absent from the the archaeological record." Indeed, Professor Rundkvist says, the kings of Scandinavia "received gold only if and when the Frankish kings allowed them to…Very probably gold could now only be had in return for an oath of fealty."[39]

This looks very like what the Messenger in *Beowulf* is foreboding. Though one wonders whether possibly the arrow of causality might have pointed the other way. If the Franks had cut off supplies a little earlier than the dates commonly suggested—and such dates are not definite—then Hygelac's raid (the date of which is also indefinite within fifteen years or so) could have been an angry *response* to the withdrawal of favour, rather than, as the poem would have it, the cause of it.

---

[39] Martin Rundkvist, "Post festum. Solid gold among the Swedes from the end of the Migration Period solidi import to the beginning of the Viking raids." Unpublished paper read at the annual meeting of the Medieval Academy of America, Minneapolis, April 12, 2003, "bled gold," "glamour," "absent" (1), "oath of fealty" (4).

But either way, when things are short, whether food or fuel or *maðmas*, what happens is that people fight all the harder for what's left of it. One very likely result of the gold shortage was to increase competition between the rival factions or dynasties within Scandinavia. The displeasure of the Merovingian was, then, one more part of the "perfect storm" of the 530s, which included (Rundkvist suggests) "the final clearing out of the Migration Period treasuries," a "central cultural trauma" from which Scandinavia took generations to recover.[40] (One might add that in a gold-shortage, a dragon-hoard from the time of wealth long ago looks very like wish-fulfilment: as longed-for and as unlikely as winning a National Lottery fortune now.)

---

40 Rundkvist, "Post festum," 2.

Chapter 4

The Non-National Epic

The Big Question: Why in England?

Fimbulwinter, crop failure, famine, plague, civil war fought to extinction, continuing vendetta between royal houses, and to cap it all, a dearth of prestige items for the ruling elites, almost as bad as having your mead-settles taken away—as Professors Herschend and Rundkvist have said in their different ways, and as corroborated by Dr. Ljungkvist, it looks very much as if the mid-sixth century was indeed a traumatic period for south and central Scandinavia.

But why should that worry an English writer a couple of centuries later? So much so that he spent a great deal of time and effort integrating many events into his story of a hero and a succession of monsters? He could after all have set his upgraded fairy-tale in England. If he wanted a location for a haunted hall called Heorot—"Hart Hall" or "Stag Hall"—he might well have had one ready to hand. As Professor Harris of Harvard has pointed out, there was a suitable location at Hartlepool, on the northeast coast of England.[1] A very suitable one, indeed, for one of the chilling aspects of the landscape of Heorot in *Beowulf* is that it is by a lake—Grendel's mother's lair is at the bottom of it—which is so feared that

---

1 See Joseph Harris, "A Note on the other Heorot," in *The Dating of Beowulf*, ed. Neidorf (Woodbridge: Boydell & Brewer, 2014), 178–90.

even a hunted animal will turn and die on the shore rather than try to swim across it. Much the same story is still told of the pools near Hartlepool called "Hell Kettles," said to be bottomless and again, shunned by animals. Not far away, moreover, is Hart Hall itself, said to be haunted by the Hart Hall Hob.[2] There is no obvious need for *Beowulf* to have a Scandinavian setting at all. So why is it there?

One common answer—implied rather than stated, as is so often the case with theories about the poem—is that it is a response to Viking Age politics in England. There is a moment in *Beowulf*, just after Wealhtheow has made her doomed attempt to protect the future of her sons, when the poet surveys the Danish hall as the retainers settle themselves for sleep, bringing out their beds and bolsters, and settling their shields and armour and helmets on the benches. He comments approvingly that the Danes were always "ready for war," whenever their lord had need of them: "that was a good people."

Professor Dorothy Whitelock (my old tutor) pointed out long ago[3] that comments of this kind were unlikely to have found a favourable reception in England during the almost three centuries of Viking wars, 789–1066, very reasonably, as one might think. Her remark was however fallen on several times by critics[4] who argued that Danes and English had often made their own accommodations during those centuries, both on the political level—like the treaty between King Alfred of Wessex and King Guthrum of East Anglia made about 880—and on the domestic level: it must be significant that our word "wife" comes from Old English *wif*, while our word

---

2 See Philip Cardew, "Grendel: Bordering the Human," in *The Shadow-Walkers: Jacob Grimm's Mythology of the Monstrous*, ed. Tom Shippey (Tempe: Arizona Center for Medieval and Renaissance Studies, 2005), 189–205.

3 In her book *The Audience of Beowulf* (Oxford: Clarendon, 1951), 24.

4 See for comment Tom Shippey, "*Beowulf*-Studies from Tolkien to Fulk," in *Old English Philology: Studies in Honour of R. D. Fulk*, ed. Leonard Neidorf, Rafael J. Pascual, and Tom Shippey (Cambridge: Brewer, 2016), 392–414 at 401.

for "husband" comes from Old Norse *hus-bondr*. So the whole point of *Beowulf*, in this view, was to celebrate Anglo-Danish harmony: it is a piece of tenth-century propaganda. (I have to remark here that one unlikely idea from the past, put forward by Levin Schücking,[5] was that the poem had been commissioned by a Danish prince of the Danelaw, *so as to teach his children Old English*: Professor Whitelock refused even to consider it, just because—so she said—this would mean that the poem had been *from the beginning* a "set-book" which young people were forced unwillingly to study.)

The tenth-century propaganda argument nevertheless fails on at least three grounds besides personal taste (which is probably why it is regularly implied rather than stated). First, there may have been "accommodations" and practical "integration"—accommodation and integration are buzz-words for modern liberal historians—but there is no other English text from the period which actually offers fulsome flattery of the Danes, like *Beowulf*, in fact just the opposite. Second, if the poem is all about Anglo-Danish integration, why are the Angles, or English, never even mentioned? And third, if the poem is a reflection of contemporary politics, why is so much of the poem about Geats, a people elsewhere all but completely forgotten in Anglo-Saxon England and certainly forming no faction in national politics?

So the question remains: what, if anything, was the link between the place of composition (England) and the setting of the poem (Scandinavia)? As so often, what we know about the poem, and what the poem actually says, appear to be completely at odds, see p. 77 above.

Answer 1: The Figure of Hengest

The only two characters in the poem who might conceivably have a link to historic England are Offa and Hengest. Offa, however, is a dead-end as regards connecting poem

---

5 See Shippey and Haarder, *Beowulf: The Critical Heritage*, 68–69, 536–42.

and real-life context. Mention of the first or Anglian Offa, the one who fought one-against-two against the *Swæfe*, could be seen as a veiled compliment to the historic eighth-century English King Offa of Mercia, creator of Offa's Dyke. But in that case one has to wonder why the compliment is not explicitly made? The poet says that the first Offa's distinguished descendants included Eomer and Garmund, both identifiable in the genealogy of the early Mercian kings, and it would seem to be an easy business to extend the comment to the first Offa's later namesake (unless of course he had not been born yet: he ruled 757–796, another argument for a date of composition for the poem in the first quarter of the eighth century).

Hengest offers a rather better potential link-up. It should be said first that his name was pronounced "Henjest," as in "hinge" or "Stonehenge"—Tolkien insisted on this, and also thought that the place-name Hincksey, just outside Oxford, might commemorate him, "Henjest's island." A further issue is that Hengest is clearly an animal-name, of which we have others in the poem: the Geatish brothers Wulf and Eofor, meaning "wolf" and "boar" respectively. Readers of *The Hobbit* will also realize that the common Anglo-Saxon name Beorn originally meant "bear." Large and dangerous animals, then, were acceptable as masculine names. In regular Old English, however—Old English being a West Germanic language—*hengest* usually (but not always) means "gelding," while in Old Norse, a North Germanic language, the related form *hestr* means "stallion." The latter is obviously a much more likely name for Heroic Age parents to give a son. This west/north difference may be significant, see further below, p. 121.

The only Hengest who appears in the PASE website's (very substantial) list of recorded and real-life Anglo-Saxon names is the ancestor of King Æthelberht of Kent, and presumably (see below) the first invader of Kent. Was he the same man as the hero of Finnsburg? Tolkien certainly thought so, adding that if we follow the evidence we should believe "that we have preserved two traditions of different adventures in the life-history of one famous adventurer."[6] By contrast Professor Woolf of St. Andrews has argued that the "historical" Hengest never existed, let alone *Beowulf*'s legendary one: he was just a "learned construct," derived by mistake from a Latin gloss.

What, then, is the evidence we should follow? Looking at the legendary side first—Professor Woolf, by the way, comments that *Beowulf* and the *Finnsburg Fragment*, "once read, cannot be unread," but he clearly wishes they could be and allows them no weight at all[7]—two Old English poems dealing with the same event and person is a unique coincidence (that makes six noted so far), and as far as Hengest goes, they agree. Hengest is the core of the "Finnsburg Episode" in *Beowulf.* He takes over at the death of Hnæf; he makes the deal with Finn; and the poet spends more than twenty lines relating the locked-in state of the surviving Half-Danes, unable to return home because of the winter storms, and Hengest's own frozen frustration at being unable to take vengeance—until spring comes, and his self-control cracks. The *Fragment*, meanwhile, is just a snapshot of the night attack and the first clashes, but it too foregrounds Hengest. After the watchman has seen flashes in the moonlight, and Hnæf has realized what's happening and called his men to arms, this poet lists the responders: Sigeferth and Eaha to one door, Ordlaf and Guthlaf to another, and then adds, line 17, *and Hengest sylf hwearf him on laste*, "and Hengest himself turned in their track." Hengest is picked out with the word "himself"—as if he is the famous one, known already. Hengest of Finnsburg was a major figure of Old English legend.

What of the other Hengest, invader of Kent? Our evidence for him comes from two sources, Bede's Latin "Ecclesiastical History of the English People," completed some time before Bede's death in 731; and the Latin "History of the Britons" written allegedly by "Nennius" a century later. It has to be said immediately that if there is one text which modern historians dislike more than *Beowulf*, it is Nennius's *History*,

---

6 Tolkien, *Finn and Hengest*, 67.

7 Woolf, "Imagining English Origins," 1.

for reasons to be explained later, see p. 116 below: still, as regards Hengest, it has to be considered as evidence, along with Bede.

Bede's story is clear: except in one point, which is however a vital one. According to him, in the year 449—at last, a date!—the "Angles or Saxons" came to Britain at the invitation of the British King Vortigern in only three ships, and were hired by the hard-pressed Britons, now abandoned by the Roman army, to defend the country against Picts and Scots. They soon call for reinforcements, and Bede contradicts himself slightly by saying that these came from "the three most formidable races of Germany"—which the Angles at least certainly weren't—that is, the Saxons, Angles, and Jutes. These then turned on the Britons, and reduced them to slavery, massacre, or flight. The Jutes, says Bede, settled in Kent, the Isle of Wight, and part of Hampshire (namely, the Meon valley, though that is a later inference). Bede also indicates the areas settled by Saxons and Angles, and says (apparently referring to the Angles) "their chieftains are said to have been the chieftains Hengist and Horsa."[8]

Nennius tells much the same story, with more detail, and very much from the point of view of the native British, whom we now call the Welsh. He says that first three *ciulae* come (the word is borrowed from the much earlier writer Gildas's *cyulis*, his rendering of Old English *ceolas* or "keels"). Then sixteen come, then forty. The leaders are Horsa and Hengest, invited as in Bede by Vortigern, and they are given the Isle of Thanet off the coast of Kent. Fighting breaks out between Britons and "barbarians"—whom Nennius identifies rather vaguely as led by "the leaders of Angeln"—with mixed results, until an attempt is made to broker peace. Both sides shall come unarmed to confirm their treaty: sitting together, "man beside man." But Hengest has told his men to hide their daggers until he calls out, "*Eu, nimet saxas!*," "Hey, draw your

---

8 Bede, *A History of the English Church and People*, trans. Leo Shirley-Price, rev. R.E. Latham (Harmondsworth: Penguin, 1968), 56 (bk. 1, chap. 15).

knives!" He makes the call, the *Saxones* draw, each man kill-ing his British opposite number, and Vortigern (whose life has been saved on Hengist's order) cedes much of southeast England to the invaders.[9] The massacre became famous in Welsh tradition as *Brad y Cyllyll Hirion*, "the Treason of the Long Knives."

One of many weak points in Nennius is that he seems unsure (or uninterested) as to whether the barbarians are Angles or Saxons, while he knows nothing of Jutes. English tradition, however, is consistent in declaring that Kent was inhabited by Jutes, and early Kentish laws are discernibly dif-ferent from the laws of other Anglo-Saxon kingdoms. But the sticking-point against identifying Bede-and-Nennius Hengest with *Beowulf*-and-Finnsburg Hengest is this: Hengest King of Kent looks like a Jute. Hengest the Half-Dane, follower of Hnæf the Scylding, is definitely fighting *against* the Jutes, very much the villains of the piece in the "Finnsburg Episode."

It is this clash of viewpoints which is resolved by the Tolk-ien theory, of "Jutes on both sides": as said above, the "Free Jutes in exile" and the "Danish-collaborator Jutes," Hengest being one of the latter. If one accepts that theory (and no-one has ever come up with a better one), then what was the situ-ation for Hengest after he had killed Finn and returned home to half-Danish Jutland. In triumph?

One might conclude that he would be deeply unpopular, in fact hated, by any of the "free Jute" faction who survived: he was responsible (in Tolkien's scenario) for the death of their last prince and the extinction of their hopes of independence. He might not have been popular with the "Half-Danes" either: his vengeance for Hnæf was delayed and dubious. In the Ger-manic world generally (in so far as there was one) he might be regarded as less than honourable. He had done a deal with the *bana* or "bane" of his lord, instead of dying with his lord like a true retainer. And having done the deal, and made a

---

9 Nennius, *Historia Brittonum*, ed. and trans. John Morris (London and Chichester: Phillimore, 1980), 26 (the keels), 34 (the *saxas*) (respectively chaps. 31, 46).

"firm compact of peace," he had then broken it. Divided loyalties and oath-breaking were the staples of Germanic legend, but that was because they were so painful, not so admirable.

Such a man might then have little option except to become a *wrǣcca*, a word which means at once "exile," "unfortunate person" (as in modern "wretch"), and "mercenary adventurer" (as in modern German *Recke*). In the *Fragment*, when young Garulf calls out to know who he's fighting, the response is, lines 24–26a: "My name is Sigeferth, a man of the Secge, a well-known *wreccea*. I have endured many woes, many hard battles." The next line-and-a-half are to say the least obscure, but to me they indicate careless indifference: footloose adventurers, living by the sword, were not people to be concerned by challenges from the young and inexperienced.

Might Finnsburg-Hengest, then, have done what it says in *Hamlet*, "sharked up a list of lawless resolutes," just three shiploads of them, to try their luck in a new country? The dates are not incompatible. If we accept that the Scylding ascendancy began in the early 400s, see p. 27 above, it might have stretched across Sjælland and Funen to the Jutes of Jutland and the partial take-over by "Half-Danes" a generation later: which would square very well wth Hengest arriving in Britain in 449. And one does have to say that the *Bad y Cyllyll Hirion* does look very like a *modus operandi*. (I refuse to remark again on "coincidence.")

Answer 2: The Figure of Hrothmund

Hengest still gets into the history books, despite all the efforts of historians to heave him out of them. Hrothmund does not. He is the most insignificant of the Scylding dynasty, mentioned only once in *Beowulf* as sitting by his brother Hrethric. In fact there is no reason for him to appear in the poem at all, unless it was felt more affecting to have two young princes threatened by a powerful cousin rather than just one. Unlike his brother, he is not mentioned in the farewell-scene between Beowulf and Hrothgar, and unlike his brother again, he has left not even a doubtful trace in Scandinavian tradition.

Yet Hrothmund is like Hengest in one way. He has a rare name, such that in all our extensive Anglo-Saxon records, there are only two Hrothmunds. Could they be the same man?

That is the opinion of Dr. Sam Newton, Director of Wuffing Education at Sutton Hoo Online, and the author of *Beowulf and the Pre-Viking Kingdom of East Anglia*, to which I am much indebted (though on one point we are in for-once friendly disagreement, see below, p. 112). Dr. Newton points out that the only other Hrothmund known—apart from a late and rather dubious "Rodmund" recorded in Domesday Book—appears in the genealogy of Ælfwald, King of East Anglia ca. 713–749. Royal genealogies are suspect for several reasons. One is that the clerics given the job of compiling them in kingdoms which had converted to Christianity had all read the first chapter of the Gospel of Matthew, which gives the genealogy of Christ in fourteen-generation units. Accordingly they were liable to try to produce their royal employers' genealogies in a fourteen-generation format, or a fourteen-generation-multiple format, the former used for Ælfwald in East Anglia, as well as kings of Essex and Kent and Deira, the latter in the twenty-eight ancestor list of the Old Norse *Ynglingatal*.[10] The trouble with a set format is that there must be a temptation to cut out names, or even more likely, to manufacture extra names to fit the pattern. Be that as it may, Hrothmund is there, fifth in line, nine generations above Ælfwald, and four generations on from the pagan god Woden, claimed as the originator of the royal line.

The appearance of Woden actually makes two more points about royal genealogies, one being that their main purpose may well have been to assert dynastic authority more than genetic fact: second in the Ælfwald line, right after Woden the god, is "Caser," a generic term for Roman of Greek Emperor— very distinguished, highly prestigious, but most unlikely as a real ancestor for a barbarian king. The other point is that it may not be generations which are being counted, but succes-

---

[10] Sam Newton, *The Origins of Beowulf and the Pre-Viking Kingdom of East Anglia* (Cambridge: Brewer, 1993), 58–60.

sions. In the distinctly Beowulfian West Saxon royal genealogies—one of them produced by a member of the royal family (it goes Beo, Scyld, Scef)—Beow is given as son of Sceldwa, but Sceldwa is son of Heremod. If one follows the hints of the poem, however, then Scyld was not the *son* of Heremod, but his successor to the throne, the king who took over after Heremod was deposed and driven out.

Many reasons for scepticism, then, about genetic facts, but as with Hengest, the dates for the two Hrothmunds are quite compatible. Nine generations, or nine reigns, counted back from Ælfwald, at say twenty years each (lives were shorter in those days, and people bred more quickly) would take us back from 713 to 533, very close to the time of the Hygelac disaster and the (theorized) Hrothulf take-over: a good time for a dispossessed prince to go on the run. Figuring another way, almost exactly halfway between Ælfwald and Hrothmund is "Wuffa," son (or successor) of Wehha. Bede, writing in the late 720s, says that Wuffa was the founder of the East Anglian line, and ever since his time the East Anglian dynasty have called themselves the *Wuffingas*. That would put Wuffa in the early 600s, a time when Anglo-Saxon kingdoms were indeed coalescing.

But what was Wuffa's real or full name: for it is clearly an "apocoristic" or short-form name, very common in Anglo-Saxon records, and still very common in modern Iceland. There, in Iceland, Guthmundr is likely to be called "Gummi" by his friends, while Thormothr will be "Tommi" and Thorbjörn "Tobbi." The convention seems to be, simplify the consonant-cluster in the middle of the name by dropping the first element, and stress the second element: so that Offa, for instance, might have been short for Os-ferhth.

It is odds-on, then, that Wuffa's real or long-form name was Wulf-something, Wulfstan or Wulfgar. And that, to Dr. Newton, raises another possibility. Was Wuffa perhaps a member of the tribe of the Wulfings, or Wylfings, mentioned twice in *Beowulf*? (Beowulf's father killed one of them, and Hrothgar paid compensation for him, in the form, of course, of *ealde madmas*, "old mathoms.") They are mentioned also in

Widsith, which says (listing them just after the "Sea-Danes"), "Hnæf [ruled] the Hocings, Helm the Wulfings."

Wealhtheow (in *Beowulf* Hrothmund's mother) is identified as soon as she appears—it is the first and only thing we are told about her, other than she is "Hrothgar's queen"—as *ides Helminga*, "the lady of the Helmings." There are only two Helminghams in England—"the home of the Helmings," or "the home of Helm's people"—one in Norfolk, and the other in Suffolk, close to Sutton Hoo and to the old royal centre of Rendlesham. Moreover, if Wealhtheow had *family* descent from Helm, according to *Widsith* ruler of the Wulfings, would that make her *tribal* designation the Wulfings? In which case there would be another possible connection between the East Anglian royal house of the seventh century, and the Danish court of the sixth.[11]

One thing about which there can be no doubt is the very strong physical and archaeological connections between East Anglia and the Beowulfian world of Scandinavia. These show up repeatedly in the famous Sutton Hoo ship-burial in Suffolk. The magnificent helmet found there—the *heregrima* or "warmask," to use the Beowulfian term—has close parallels with helmets found in similar burials in Sweden, at Vendel and Valsgärde. So does the great gold buckle with its niello ornament. The most striking similarity is the "dancing warriors" design on the Sutton Hoo helmet, so similar to a fragment of bronze foil found in Sweden that they may have come from the same workshop: it was found in the mound once conjectured to be the burial-mound of Ongentheow. A mound close by, and assigned long ago to Eadgils, the "last man standing" in *Beowulf*, also contains a gold fragment technically similar to the jewellery of Sutton Hoo.[12] All these finds connect the Wuffings with Sweden rather than Denmark, but this may be because, in the early seventh century, the time of Sutton

---

11 See again Newton, *The Origins of Beowulf*, 105–6 (Wuffings) and 126–27 (Helmings).

12 Newton, *The Origins of Beowulf*, 110–13 (helmet, foil, jewellery).

Hoo, East Anglia and Sweden were the centres of wealth for England and Scandinavia.

Kings of East Anglia were, then, at least aware of Scandinavia and in what one might call "*mathom*-contact" with it, long before the Vikings: as is indeed claimed by the title of Dr. Newton's book.

Answer 3: All Those Hrethlings

The Suffolk connection to *Beowulf* is debatable, and indeed it has been debated. Dr. Newton is a Suffolk man, while the Shippeys, by contrast, come ancestrally from North Yorkshire. The rival claims of these two areas have been debated in front of audiences in Suffolk and in Yorkshire, and the results, as might have been expected, were indecisive, affected by local patriotism (not to mention audiences packed with cousins and relatives). In the interest of scholarly integrity I should state here that there is one piece of evidence which strongly favours Suffolk, and that is the word *mor*, or "moor."

In modern English, this usually means "waste upland," as in Dartmoor or Exmoor or the North York Moors. Place-names like Frogmore (found many times in England) however indicate an alternative meaning, "waste marshland." This is what the word means in *Beowulf*, where it occurs six times, including the compound word *mor-hop*, "remote place in a moor," clearly the same (in the poet's mind) as *fen-hop*, "remote place in a fen." The fact that, to the poet, *mor = fen*, argues strongly for flatland like Suffolk as a place of origin. The great Beowulf scholar of the nineteenth century, Karl Viktor Müllenhoff, was indeed convinced the poem came from his own "narrow homeland" of Dithmarschen, or the Ditmarsh, just south of the river Eider, and felt a strong connection also to the character Widsith, who self-identifies as a Myrging, one of "the Mire-people."[13] But he may have picked the wrong mire: local patriotism has been a force in *Beowulf*-studies for a long time.

---

13 Shippey and Haarder, *Beowulf: The Critical Heritage*, 38–41.

That said, however, is there a case for looking at North Yorkshire as one more connecting link to the poem?

The missing Beowulfian tribe in England has to be Beowulf's own people, the Geats (*Geatas*), mostly forgotten, and regularly confused with the Jutes (*Eotan*). What trace, if any, remains of them? There used to be, in England, a shire which has long since disappeared from the administrative map: Gillingshire, which once ran from East Gilling east of York to West Gilling north of Richmond. There is general agreement that this was once the area mentioned by Bede as *Ingetlingum*. Might this mean, the home of the Geat-lings, the "little Geats"? Probably not. More likely it means, "the home of the followers of Getla." On the other hand, Getla must derive from *Geat-ila or *Gaut-ila, in other words Geat + a regular diminutive (Attila the Hun got his name, unlikely as it seems, from Gothic *atta*, "father" + diminutive *-ila*, so "little father" or "daddy": Tolkien was thrilled at the revelation).

There the matter might rest if not for two things: the researches of Tolkien's Leeds predecessor, Frederick Moorman, and a surprising omission from the statistics of PASE. Moorman was Professor of English Language at the Yorkshire College, which became the University of Leeds, from 1912 to 1918—it was his death which presumably allowed the University to promote Tolkien from Reader to Professor, and it should be recorded that he died like a hero, attempting to save a child from drowning in the River Skirfare. (It is well-known in the north that trying to save anyone from a river will arouse the vengeance of the river-hag, be she Peg Powler of the Tees or Jenny Greenteeth of the Ribble. Only the likes of Tom Bombadil can do that with impunity.)

Moorman had one advantage over later scholars, which was that he knew Yorkshire well, though he was not uninfluenced by local patriotism. Some of the place-names he collected in a 1915 essay, as proof of knowledge of "Teutonic saga," have not stood the test of time.[14] Beeston in Leeds has

---

14 Frederick Moorman, "English Place-Names and Teutonic Sagas," *Essays and Studies* 5 (1915): 75–103.

nothing to do with Beowulf, but comes from Old English *beos-tun*, "the place where reeds grow," and Grindale has nothing to do with Grendel, but meant just "green valley." Romanby and Rogerthorpe meanwhile derive from the fairly common Old Norse names Hromundr and Hrothgeirr—though these may have been Viking Age repronunciations of earlier Hroth-mund and Hrothgar, which is in fact what has happened with the Gillings: in Bede's pronunciation they would have been *Yelling or *Yetling.

Moorman was quite right about two more names, how-ever, and these are especially surprising. The name of Hrethel, in *Beowulf* the grandfather of the Geatish royal house, is absolutely unknown in any Old English or Old Norse record—except in Yorkshire, where Riddlesden (in Domesday Book *Redelesden*) once meant "Hrethel's valley," and Rillington (DB *Redlintone*), right in the middle of Gillingshire, preserves the Beowulfian word *Hrethling*.[15] So *someone* remembered the Hrethlings.

Meanwhile, as remarked already, PASE preserves few traces of the five names in the Geatish royal dynasty accord-ing to *Beowulf*, Hrethel, Herebeald, Hæthcyn, Hygelac and Heardred, the scores for them being respectively 0, 4, 0, 2, and 4, and some of these being overcounted: PASE counts occurrences, not people, and three of the Herebealds recorded, all moneyers of the mid-ninth century, are probably the same person—though the fourth was abbot of Tynemouth more than a century earlier. Likewise PASE's two Hyglacs are probably the same person, a lector at York ca. 800 (and like Herebeald abbot of Tynemouth, and Heardred bishop of Hex-ham, from the northeast of England)

PASE, however, not only does not count names from *Beow-ulf*, on the logical ground that these may not have been real people, it also (for some reason) did not take in the 2819 names recorded in the *Northumbrian Liber Vitae*, the old core of the Durham *Liber Vitae*, a list of members and benefactors of the

---

15 Eilert Ekwall, *The Concise Oxford Dictionary of English Place-Names*, 4th ed. (Oxford: Clarendon, 1960), 386, 387 respectively.

church in Durham. Though this is a much smaller corpus than PASE's, the scores are very different. Not only does it have the very rare name Beowulf (a monk written down as "Biuuulf," note the familiar problem with the letter -w),[16] but it contains four Hygelacs, eight Herebealds, and eleven Heardreds, as well as sixteen Ingelds: and all these *are* different people.

Professor Neidorf's study of names in the *NLV*[17] notes scrupulously that since the name-elements Here- and Heard-, -beald and -red, are all common, they are bound to produce Herebealds and Heardreds through random combination: but statistically speaking, one would think, not in such numbers. And this argument does not apply to the name Hygelac. If (yet again) we put "coincidence" aside, it seems that in the north-east of England, from which the Durham community drew its members and benefactors, including Gillingshire some twenty miles to the south, there were families which (like Dr. Hammer's Bavarians remembering Hnæf and Hoc) generation after generation named their sons in memory of Geatish royals, using names which rarely if ever show up anywhere else.

A Hypothesis, and "the Age of Arthur"

The hypothesis arises naturally from the remarks above about Hengest, Hrothmund, and the Hrethling names, and it is quite a simple one: namely, that in the general turmoil which forms the background of the main story of *Beowulf*, the losers in all the dynastic strife decided to cut their losses and emigrate to England: where, however, their descendants did not forget the various family traumas, but made them part of legendary or historical tradition (which earlier ages did not distinguish as we do).

---

16 PASE also has a "Beulf," a name from Dorset recorded in Domesday Book.

17 Leonard Neidorf, "Beowulf before *Beowulf*: Anglo-Saxon Anthroponymy and Heroic Legend," *Review of English Studies* 64 (2012): 553–73 at 557–58.

Hengest the Jute, to whom the whole seaboard from Jutland to Frisia is now a no-go area, leads his "list of lawless resolutes" to the conquest of Kent. Hrothmund the Dane, in danger of falling victim like his brother Hrethric to his powerful cousin Hrothulf, leads his supporters to East Anglia, where his descendants found the Wuffing dynasty. Members of the Geats, with very little to hope for from a coming Swedish takeover, head for North Yorkshire. All these events take place at different dates, but within a recognizable time-frame, *very* approximately 440–550: the heart of the "Dark Age" for Northwest Europe, and even worse, if one is considering the English situation, containing within it the "Age of Arthur."

It's already been remarked that if there is one text which historians like even less than *Beowulf*, it is Nennius's *Historia Brittonum*, the earliest shoot of the whole tree of Arthur-tales. And if there is one phrase they dislike even more than "Dark Age," it is "Age of Arthur." Still, that is where we are: and worse still, there are some slight connections between the *Beowulf*-scenario and what little we know of Arthur.

One is the "dust veil" of 536. It was realized only recently[18] that there is a reference to this in Gildas's *De excidio et conquestu Britanniae*, "On the Downfall and Conquest of Britain," our only contemporary account of the most important event in British history—the change from Roman Britannia to *Engla-land*, "the land of the English"—and one regarded by historians with reserve, if not the downright loathing reserved for his follower Nennius. In chapter 93 of his bad-tempered tract, Gildas refers to the "dense cloud and black night" which looms "over the whole island." He ascribes this to sin (like everything else), but this is surely the "dust veil" already mentioned of 536, noted world-wide, and especially ruinous for Scandinavia, see p. 74 above.

Gildas was then most likely writing in 536, and Professor Breeze of Navarre argues that since Gildas does not mention the later *mortalitas* or famine, he must have been writ-

---

18 By David Woods; see for details and discussion Breeze, *British Battles*, 5–7.

ing before that became apparent, therefore early in the year. In which case, Gildas's very definite dating (chap. 26) of the *obsessio montis Badonici* or "siege of Mount Badon" to forty-three years earlier (the date of his own birth) gives us a date for that event, a major win for the Britons against the invaders, of 493: which agrees exactly with Bede's dating.

The Mount Badon victory is now regularly ascribed to Arthur in films and historical novels, but in fact Gildas says nothing about him. Nevertheless Arthur is active at about this time: the *Annales Cambriae* record his death as taking place at *Camlann*, the old Roman fort of *Cambogalanna* on Hadrian's Wall, now Housesteads, in 537. Breeze suggests that Arthur owes his fame (and in the end, very likely his death) to a successful career of cattle-raiding in the north of England during the post-536 famine.[19] But whatever one thinks of Arthur, this is the disaster-era for both Britain and Scandinavia: also, the era of opportunity for violent change.

I attempt therefore to interleave what dates we know into a sequence for both areas and both historico-legendary traditions, urging all readers to recognize that most of the dates are approximate to say the least. If this seems an excessively bold exercise—as it is by timid academic standards—I can plead only that Tolkien (who thought that his name derived from German *tollkühn*, "foolhardy") was a great deal bolder. He devised chronologies for everything,[20] and kept adjusting them. Setting them out fair and square, the way hobbits like their books, at least enables one to see if everything fits: and in the case of *Beowulf*, I think it does.

Here, then, is a dual chronology for the Age of Hygelac / the Age of Arthur: events in Britain are indented. (It should be obvious that all dates are approximate, dubious, or both. The question is whether they are compatible.)

---

19 See Breeze, *British Battles*, 11–24, summary on 23.

20 For Tolkien chronologies, with discussion, see *Beowulf: A Translation and Commentary*, 321–33, and *Finn and Hengest*, 165–67.

Dates	Events in Scandinavia (and broader)	Events in Britain
400 onwards	The Scyldings under King Healfdene extend their control from Lejre towards Jutland	
410		The Romans leave Britain. Rome itself is sacked by the Goths
ca. 440	The Fight at Finnsburg	
449		The *adventus Saxonum*, or "coming of the Saxons" to Britain, with Hengest the Jute in the lead
493		Major defeat of the "Saxons" at Mount Badon
510 onwards		The ascendancy of Arthur
520 onwards	The long vendetta between Swedish and Geatish royal houses (for which see sequence of events on pp. 56–57 above)	
ca. 530	The Hygelac disaster in the Netherlands	
530 onwards	The ascendancy of Hrothulf: the flight of Hrothmund	
536	The dust-veil and following famine.	Gildas writes his tract
537		The death of Arthur
ca. 540	The death of Hrothulf and extinction of the Scyldings	

Dates	Events in Scandinavia (and broader)	Events in Britain
ca. 540	Signs of transfer of power in Östergotland: probable Swedish victory and flight of Geatish elites	
597		Arrival of St. Augustine and his missionaries in Canterbury: end of the era of near-total illiteracy in Britain

About the only thing certain in all this is that it was a long century of trouble on both sides of the North Sea, as the losers in the east looked for opportunities in the west. We know nothing about what was happening in the east, except from *Beowulf*, and from archaeology. But what was happening in the west, in Britain and especially in England?

There are two schools of thought here, one old, one new. The old one said, effectively, that for many years southern Britain underwent a period of what we would now call "ethnic cleansing," as a mass migration of Angles, Saxons, and Jutes drove out the native Britons and established their own kingdoms. The new one says—in line with the modern "Rome never fell" theory—that there was no mass migration, but a fairly peaceful accommodation and resettlement of English-speakers, who eventually became dominant in the east of the island.

The old one perhaps took Gildas too literally. He was quite clear about what happened: "All the major towns were laid low...laid low, too, all the inhabitants...There was no burial to be had except in the ruins of houses and the bellies of beasts and birds." Some were killed, some enslaved, some emigrated "for lands beyond the sea."[21] Eventually some put

---

21 Chap. 24/3 of Gildas, *The Ruin of Britain*, ed. Winterbottom, 27.

up a fight, but their efforts were bedevilled by civil war and the rise of tyrants and warlords—these last being Gildas's real targets. Gildas is now regularly put aside by historians, who point to (some) archaeological evidence of continuity, even in major towns and cities.

On the other hand, he is our only source who was living at the time. The archaeologist Heinrich Härke has remarked sardonically that opinions are formed not on the evidence, but on historians' own differing experiences. German historians, who have known mass flight from east to west even in their own time, find mass migration and mass flight not incredible. British historians, familiar from their own history in India and Africa with the idea of elites installing themselves as a ruling class with little population disturbance, find the elite takeover theory much more natural.

There is one fact, however, which is very hard for the new school of thought to explain away, and that is, wholesale language change. In the year 400 the island of Britain spoke the Celtic language Old British, in different dialects, from end to end. By 600 most of it spoke English, again in different dialects. Elite takeovers, like the British conquest of India, or closer to home the Norman Conquest of 1066, do not create mass language change. Härke suggests, noting also major changes in law, pottery, burial customs, and culture—and by this time being downright sarcastic—that perhaps the new school of thought believes that there was no mass migration of Germanic-speakers, only of "Germanic life-style advisers," presumably including language-teachers.[22]

One might note also that (as Gildas hints) there definitely was another mass migration, this time of Britons leaving the southwest of England and settling in what is now Bretagne or Brittany: where indeed there was another total language replacement, from Vulgar Latin (the ancestor of modern

22 Respectively Heinrich Härke, "Archaeologists and Migrations: A Problem of Attitude?," *Current Anthropology* 39, no. 1 (1998): 19–24 at 21, and Härke, "The Debate on Migration and Identity in Europe," *Antiquity* 78 (2004): 453–56 at 455.

French) to Breton (a language related to modern Welsh and more closely related to modern-era Cornish).

There is a further point about language-evidence, which takes us back to *Beowulf*, Scandinavia, and especially to Hengest, Hrothmund, and all those Hrethling names. This is that Old English is a rather strange language, compared to its Germanic relatives. One particular oddity is that it has two separate sets of words for "to be." One set, in the present tense singular, goes *ic beo, þu bist, he/heo/hit biþ*, quite like (two times out of three) modern German *ich bin, du bist, er/ sie/es ist*. This has not quite died out in modern English, at least in the southwest, "I be, she be" etc., but it identifies Old English as belonging to the West Germanic group, which includes German, Dutch, Flemish, Frisian, and Afrikaans. Old English, however, also said *ic eom, þu eart, he/heo/hit is*, what we say nowadays and much closer to Old Norse, *ek em, þu ert, hann/honn/þat er*. This by contrast identifies Old English as belonging to the North Germanic group, which consists of all the Scandinavian languages.

So which is it, West or North? The true answer, according to Professor Nielsen of Aarhus, is that Old English is fundamentally a West Germanic language, but that the early Anglo-Saxon settlers of the fifth and sixth centuries "had links to both the north and the south in *Germania* prior to their invasion of Britain."[23] (One might note that if Hengest meant "stallion," not "gelding," then that on the whole looks like early North rather than early West Germanic, Jutish rather than Saxon.) We know that modern English was affected from the tenth century on by Old Norse speakers, the incomers of the Viking Age. But the signs detected by Professor Nielsen come from much earlier, from before Old English started to be written.

This may not be completely surprising. If one thinks of Angles, Saxons, and Jutes, the Saxons were well within the

---

23 Hans Frede Nielsen, *The Continental Backgrounds of English and its Insular Development until 1154* (Odense: Odense University Press, 1998), 79.

West Germanic range, the Jutes were north of the present Danish/German border, and so probably in the North Germanic range, but the Angles were just to the south of that border, and so on the cusp of the language-division—which, back in the sixth century, must have been quite hard to discern. It's odd that even King Alfred, king of the West *Saxons*, and with a mother who was a Hampshire *Jute*, nevertheless always called his language *englisc*, never *seaxisc*, and claimed the right to rule *Angelcynn*: in some way the Angles seem to have gained a kind of non-political hegemony over the descendants of their old neighbours on the Continent.

Nevertheless the gist of what has just been said is that the sixth-century invaders of England came to a now-unrecognized extent from what would become Scandinavia: and that is why the original audience of *Beowulf* was interested in Scandinavian history. It was their history too.

And Another Question Answered

Beowulf answers another question which isn't often asked. That is: why were the Vikings, when they turned up in the late eighth century on the shores of England, such a shock? They struck the famous monastery of St. Cuthbert, on its tidal island off the northeast coast of England, on June 8, 793, an event generally regarded as having inaugurated the Viking Age. It was the Pearl Harbor of the Dark Ages. No-one was expecting it. Alcuin, a Yorkshire scholar later headhunted to join Charlemagne's scriptorium in France wrote to his then-employer King Ethelred of Northumbria:

> It is some three hundred and fifty years that we and our forefathers have inhabited this lovely land, and never before in Britain has such a terror appeared as this we have now suffered at the hands of the heathen. Nor was it thought possible that such an inroad from the sea could be made.[24]

---

24 Dorothy Whitelock, ed. and trans., *English Historical Documents: Vol. 1, c. 500-1042* (London: Oxford University Press, 1969), 776.

Never before? Not thought possible? Alcuin—his real name was *Alhwini, usual trouble with -w, and it means "friend of the (heathen) temple," though he perhaps did not know that—seems to have forgotten everything about his own history. "Three hundred and fifty years" back from 793 takes us to 443, very close to the date of the "coming of the Saxons" according to Bede, and that "coming," according to Gildas and Nennius, involved just the kind of attacks that took Alcuin so badly by surprise. Saxon raids from the sea had moreover been commonplace back in the Roman period—the Romans built signal stations all along the east coast to watch out for them and created a special military officer in charge of defences, the *comes littoris saxonici*, "the count of the Saxon shore." So why was Alcuin so shocked?

Because the raids had stopped. The real surprise is not the resumption, but the cessation. We don't know how long this period of security lasted, and obviously Alcuin didn't either, but the arrival of incomers from across the sea may well have continued for a hundred years after 449 (according to Dr. Härke's logistical calculations).[25] But that takes us once again to the mid-sixth century, the period when—as said above, p. 71—"the roof fell in" for Scandinavia, or, to repeat Professor Herschend's words, "the region went down to hell."

The Hygelac disaster; the great famine; the family-suicide of the Scyldings in Denmark; the elimination of the Hrethlings in Gothland; Athils the Scylfing as last man standing… All this might well lead to a serious drop in resources, and quite possibly also, a serious failure of confidence among the warlike elites of Scandinavia. The peace which left Alcuin so unprepared, then, was a peace of poverty and exhaustion. It took generations for Scandinavia to recover—and then (as indicated by the affair at Portland, see p. 11 above) the new

---

25 In "Anglo-Saxon Immigration and Ethnogenesis," *Medieval Archaeology* 55, no. 1 (November 2011): 1–28. Härke suggests that an immigration of up to 100,000 persons would have been possible, over time, which is compatible with DNA evidence.

expansion may well have taken off from Norway, thinly popu-
lated but mercifully unaffected by the turmoil further south.

That, however, is another story, of which the *Beowulf*-poet,
in most modern opinions, could have no idea.[26] Just the
same, his story explains a great deal about the Dark Age,
and the Heroic Age. It deserves to be understood, and taken
seriously—whatever Tolkien may have said, and later (I feel)
regretted.

---

26 For the case for dating composition of the poem to well before
the Viking Age, see R. D. Fulk, "Review Article: Dating *Beowulf*
to the Viking Age," *Philological Quarterly* 61 (1982): 341–57; *The
Dating of Beowulf*, ed. Neidorf, *passim*; and Shippey, "*Beowulf*-
Studies," esp. 399–403.

Further Reading

Bjork, Robert E., and John D. Niles, eds. *A Beowulf Handbook*. Lincoln: University of Nebraska Press, 1997.

> This contains eighteen scholarly articles on topics such as style, sources, social milieu.

Hedeager, Lotte. *Iron-Age Societies: From Tribe to State in Northern Europe, 500 BC to 700 AD*. Translated by John Hines. Oxford: Blackwell, 1992

> As the sub-title indicates, this looks at the process of centralising control described at the start of this book, with special reference to Denmark.

Herschend, Frands. *The Idea of the Good in Late Iron Age Society*. Uppsala: Uppsala universitet, Institutionen för arkeologi och antik historia, 1998.

> Centres on the idea of the hall as social space, and uses *Beowulf* (among much else) in discussion of "model behaviour" among the pagan upper classes of early Scandinavia. Available online at https://www.arkeologi.uu.se/digitalAssets/483/c_483918-l_3-k_opia15.pdf.

——— . *The Early Iron Age in South Scandinavia: Social Order in Settlement and Landscape*. Uppsala: Uppsala universitet, Institutionen för arkeologi och antik historia, 2009.

> The best survey of the real situation in pre-Viking Denmark and South Sweden. Note especially the chapter on "The Landscape of Warfare," 329–86. Also available online at http://uu.diva-portal.org/smash/record.jsf?pid=diva2%3A287406&dswid=5503.

Niles, John D., and Marijane Osborn, eds. *Beowulf and Lejre.* Tempe: Arizona Center for Medieval and Renaissance Studies, 2007.

> This includes Professor Christensen's accounts of the archaeology, up to 2005, as well as a long section by the editors on "*Beowulf* and Lejre," and another containing "Medieval Sources" for the "Legend."

Price, Neil. *The Children of Ash and Elm: A History of the Vikings.* London: Allen Lane, 2020.

> It's what it says, but Professor Price argues that you cannot understand the Vikings without understanding their traumatic prehistory, which occupies much of the first 100+ pages.

Rundkvist, Martin. *Mead-Halls of the Eastern Geats: Elite Settlements and Political Geography AD 375–1000 in Östergötland, Sweden.* Stockholm: Kungl. Vitterhets historie och antikvitets akademien, 2011.

> Closely focused on a vital area for *Beowulf*, with chapters 4 and 5 straddling the vital period of the mid-sixth century. Later investigations have also proved successful, see note 24 on p. 75.

The Saga of King Hrolf Kraki. Translated by Jesse L. Byock. London: Penguin, 1998.

> The saga itself is late, confused, and badly-told, but it is in a way, "*Beowulf*: the sequel." It follows the career of King Hrolf (the Hrothulf of the poem), and features a Beowulf-analogue in the hero Böthvar "Little Bear" Bjarki, a skin-changer like Beorn in *The Hobbit.*

Tolkien, J. R. R. *Finn and Hengest: The Fragment and the Episode.* Edited by A. J. Bliss. Boston: Houghton Mifflin, 1983.

> The clearest demonstration of Tolkien's belief in the historical value of *Beowulf*, and the "Finnsburg Fragment." Start with the "Reconstruction" on pp. 159–62.

——— . *Beowulf: A Translation and Commentary, Together with "Sellic Spell"*. Edited by Christopher Tolkien. London: Harper-Collins, 2014.

> The "Commentary" regrettably only goes up to line 1857, but is full of original ideas. "Sellic Spell" (i.e., "Wonder-tale") is Tolkien's reconstruction of what he thought was the fairy-tale which underlies the poem.

Printed and bound by CPI Group (UK) Ltd, Croydon, CR0 4YY

06/05/2024

14498207-0001